Emerson's Science
of the Spirit

Emerson's Science of the Spirit

•

A Visual Interpretation of Emerson's Natural History of Intellect

Bruce K. Kirchoff

Tellus Books
Mebane, NC

TELLUS BOOKS

Copyright © 2008 by Bruce K. Kirchoff

Published in the United States by Tellus Books, an imprint of
Metis, LLC
tellusbooks@metisllc.com

9 8 7 6 5 4 3 2 1

First Edition
Printed in the United States of America

Library of Congress Control Number: 2008911362

Kirchoff, Bruce K. 1952 —
Emerson's Science of the Spirit: A Visual Interpretation of
Emerson's Natural History of Intellect / Bruce K. Kirchoff.
– 1st TELLUS BOOKS

ISBN 978-0-9822715-0-6

In all sciences the student is discovering that nature, as he calls it, is always working, in wholes and in every detail, after the laws of the human mind. . . . It is not then cities or mountains, or animals, or globes that any longer command us, but only man; not the fact but so much of man as is in the fact.

Emerson

Contents

Preface

As I write this, the financial markets are in free fall and the economic future of the world seems uncertain. It is natural at times like these to turn inward, to withdraw from the world and take stock of those things that are most important to us. There is no better guide on this path than Emerson.

This book is an exploration of Ralph Waldo Emerson's last, great work *Natural History of Intellect*. It is an attempt to make the deeper meaning of the work accessible through visual and written commentaries on the text. It also contains the text of the *Natural History* as it appeared in the Riverside Press edition of Emerson's complete works (1893–1899).[1] Though a new discovered version of this work has been published,[2] the Riverside edition remains a good guide to Emerson's mature thought.

The Natural History is the final fruit of Emerson's intellectual labor. It is his masterwork, though it remained unpublished in his lifetime. Although it was never published, it was twice presented to audiences through the auspices of the Harvard University Lectures, the precursor of the Graduate School founded in 1872. In both 1870 and 1871 Emerson gave a course of 18 lectures (three per week) under this title.

By the end of the 1871 lectures Emerson was exhausted. He was 68 years old, and the pace of the lectures as well as the necessity of traveling from Concord to Cambridge three times a week had greatly tired him. In their final weeks the frequency of the lectures was accelerated so that they could be concluded more rapidly. As soon as they were done, Emerson was whisked away by friends for a tour of the West, relaxation and rest. It was on this tour, in the area of California that would become Yosemite National Park, that he met John Muir. Muir was a contemporary of Emerson's, and a writer whose thought complements that of the great man. On May 5, 1871 when these two great souls met, Muir was thirty three years old and working in a sawmill that he had built.[3] This book is a much delayed fruit of that meeting.

Muir's view of Nature is a wonderful complement to Emerson's. To both men Nature is a revelation of the divine, but where Emerson sees Nature as a signpost, for Muir it is alive with exhilaration.

One of the most beautiful and exhilarating storms I ever enjoyed in the Sierra occurred in December, 1874, when I happened to be exploring one of the tributary valleys of the Yuba River. The sky and the ground and the trees had been thoroughly rain–washed and were dry again. The day was intensely pure, one of those incomparable bits of California winter, warm and balmy and full of white sparkling sunshine, redolent of all the purest influences of the spring, and at the same time enlivened with one of the most bracing wind–storms conceivable. Instead of camping out, as I usually do, I then chanced to be stopping at the house of a friend. But when the storm began to sound, I lost no time in pushing out into the woods to enjoy it. For on such occasions Nature has always something rare to show us, and the danger to life and limb is hardly greater than one would experience crouching deprecatingly beneath a roof.

[. . .]

Toward midday, after a long, tingling scramble through copses of hazel and ceanothus, I gained the summit of the highest ridge in the neighborhood; and then it occurred to me that it would be a fine thing to climb one of the trees to obtain a wider outlook and get my ear close to the Æolian music of its topmost needles. . . . After cautiously casting about, I made choice of the tallest of a group of Douglas Spruces that were growing close together like a tuft of grass, no one of which seemed likely to fall unless all the rest fell with it. . . . Being accustomed to climb trees in making botanical studies, I experienced no difficulty in reaching the top of this one, and never before did I enjoy so noble an exhilaration of motion. The slender tops fairly flapped and swished in the passionate torrent, bending and swirling backward and forward, round and round, tracing indescribable combinations of vertical and horizontal curves, while I clung with muscles firm braced, like a bobo–link on a reed.

In its widest sweeps my tree–top described an arc of from twenty to thirty degrees, but I felt sure of its elastic temper, having seen others of the same species still more severely tried — bent almost to the ground indeed, in heavy snows — without breaking a fiber. I was therefore safe, and free to take the wind into my pulses and enjoy the excited forest from my superb outlook. The view from here must be extremely beautiful in any weather. Now my eye roved over the piny hills and dales as over fields of waving grain, and felt the light running in ripples and broad swelling undulations across the valleys from ridge to ridge, as the shining foliage was stirred by corresponding waves of air.[4]

The photographs that illuminate the text were taken mainly in Sequoia National Park during October 2005, though a few were taken in August, October and December 2007 both in Sequoia and Yosemite National Parks. The chief subject is *Sequoiadendron giganteum*, the giant sequoia of the Sierra Nevada, one of the most remarkable living organisms in the world. The book is linked to John Muir through this setting, and these trees. Here is his description of the species.

So exquisitely harmonious and finely balanced are even the very mightiest of these monarchs of the woods in all their proportions and circumstances there never is anything overgrown or monstrous–looking about them. On coming in sight of them for the first time, you are likely to say, "Oh, see what beautiful, noble–looking trees are towering there among the firs and pines!"—their grandeur being in the mean time in great part invisible, but to the living eye it will be manifested sooner or later, stealing slowly on the senses, like the grandeur of Niagara, or the lofty Yosemite domes. Their great size is hidden from the inexperienced observer as long as they are seen at a distance in one harmonious view.

When, however, you approach them and walk round them, you begin to wonder at their colossal size and seek a measuring–rod. These giants bulge considerably at the base, but not more than is required for beauty and safety; and the only reason that this bulging seems in some cases excessive is that only a comparatively small section of the shaft is seen at once in near views. One that I measured in the King's River forest was 25 feet in diameter at the ground, and 10 feet in diameter 200 feet above the ground, showing that the taper of the trunk as a whole is charmingly fine. And when you stand back far enough to see the massive columns from the swelling instep to the lofty summit dissolving in a dome of verdure, you rejoice in the unrivaled display of combined grandeur and beauty. About a hundred feet or more of the trunk is usually branchless, but its massive simplicity is relieved by the bark furrows, which instead of making an irregular network run evenly parallel, like the fluting of an architectural column, and to some extent by tufts of slender sprays that wave lightly in the winds and cast flecks of shade, seeming to have been pinned on here and there for the sake of beauty only. The young trees have slender simple branches down to the ground, put on with strict regularity, sharply aspiring at the top, horizontal about half–way down, and drooping in handsome curves at the base. By the time the sapling is five or six hundred years old this spiry, feathery, juvenile habit merges into the firm, rounded dome form of middle age, which in turn takes on the eccentric picturesqueness of old age. No other tree in the Sierra forest has foliage so densely massed or presents outlines so firmly drawn and so steadily subordinate to a special type. A knotty ungovernable–looking branch five to eight feet thick may be seen pushing out abruptly from the smooth trunk, as if sure to throw the regular curve into confusion, but as soon as the general outline is reached it stops short and dissolves in spreading bosses of law–abiding sprays, just as if every tree were growing beneath some huge, invisible bell–glass, against whose sides every branch was being pressed and molded, yet somehow indulging in so many small departures from the regular form that there is still an appearance of freedom.[5]

About This Book

This book is a doorway to that "unknown country" of which Emerson speaks, and which Muir seeks through his experience of Nature. Like all doors, this one does not open on its own. We must choose to go through. A sunlit landscape may appear on the other side, but if we do not go though the experience of the sun itself will remain unknown. Our experience of that country must be born through our own effort. There is no other way.

Each page of the book is a meditation on a phrase from Emerson's text. The phrases can be read quickly to give an overview of the work, but each requires quiet contemplation to bring out its deeper significance. The images were chosen to help with this. Each one repeats the meaning of the text with which it is paired. The meaning is always there, though it often requires quiet contemplation to bring it out.

Success with the book will take time. Emerson's text is rich with meaning, and Nature has so much to offer that only a small portion can be assimilated in any one sitting. The spirit is not stingy with it gifts. It delivers a torrent. Do not underestimate the task of accepting it. It takes courage and perseverance. There is a depth in Nature, and in Emerson, that defies intellectual understanding. Understanding is only the first step on the journey. The "unknown country" does not lend itself to description, or intellectual thought. Art is a better guide. Coupled with the quotes, the images can lead us to realms whose content cannot easily be expressed in words. If we try to express these qualities prematurely, we will see our experience change into something quite different. Rather than opening, the door will slowly close. It is wiser to treasure the experiences, to hold them in our hearts in quiet contemplation. Eventually, we will find the words. They should never be forced.

Acknowledgements

First and foremost I thank Stuart–Sinclear Weeks, who set me on this path. The path itself was illuminated by my lifelong study of the works of Rudolf Steiner. I find his early philosophical works to be indispensable for understanding Emerson. I owe them both a debt that I can only repay through love.

Although I have not given her the first place in these acknowledgements, without the love and support of my wife, Mary Dee Kirchoff, I would be less myself and have been less able to complete this project. What we mean to and for each other cannot easily be put into words.

Support for the 2005 trip to Sequoia National Park came from Rancho Santa Ana Botanical Garden. They allowed me to visit the park during a trip to the Garden to present a lecture and work with the scientific staff. I am grateful for the opportunity they provided.

Bruce K. Kirchoff
November 2008

[1] Ralph Waldo Emerson and James Elliott Cabot, *Emerson's Complete Works,* (Boston: The Riverside Press, Houghton, Mifflin Co., 1893–1899), vol. 12. — The Centenary edition of the Emerson's complete works contains additional essays under the heading of *Natural History of Intellect*. What is reproduced here is the first of these, *Powers and Laws of Thought*. Ralph Waldo Emerson and Edward Waldo Emerson, *The Complete Works of Ralph Waldo Emerson* (New York: Houghton Mifflin Co., Centenary Edition, 1903–1921).
[2] Maurice York and Rick Spaulding, *Natural History of the Intellect: The Last Lectures of Ralph Waldo Emerson* (Chicago: Wrightwood Press, 2008).
[3] William Frederic Badè, *The Life and Letters of John Muir* (Boston: The Riverside Press, Houghton, Mifflin and Co., 1924), vol. 1.
[4] John Muir, *The Mountains of California* (De Vinne Press, New York, 1894).
[5] Ibid.

Emerson's Science of the Spirit

Mind

I believe in the existence of the material world as the expression of the spiritual or the real, and in the impenetrable mystery which hides (and hides through absolute transparency) the mental nature . . . .

Every object in nature is a word to signify some fact in the mind. But when that fact is not yet put into English words, when I look at the tree or the river and have not yet definitely made out what they would say to me, they are by no means unimpressive. I wait for them, I enjoy them before they yet speak. I feel as if I stood by an ambassador charged with the message of his king, which he does not deliver because the hour when he should say it is not yet arrived.

Whilst we converse with truths as thoughts, they exist also as plastic forces; as the soul of a man, the soul of a plant, the genius or constitution of any part of nature, which makes it what it is. The thought which was in the world, part and parcel of the world, has disengaged itself and taken an independent existence.

I wish to know the laws of this wonderful power, that I may domesticate it. I observe with curiosity its risings and settings, illumination and eclipse; its obstructions and its provocations, that I may learn to live with it wisely, court its aid, catch sight of its splendor, feel its approach, hear and save its oracles and obey them.

In my thought I seem to stand on the bank of a river and watch the endless flow of the stream, floating objects of all shapes, colors and natures; nor can I much detain them as they pass, except by running beside them a little way along the bank. But whence they come or whither they go is not told me. Only I have a suspicion that, as geologists say every river makes its own valley, so does this mystic stream. It makes its valley, makes its banks and makes perhaps the observer too.

Who has found the boundaries of human intelligence? Who has made a chart of its channel or approached the fountain of this wonderful Nile?

Being

To Be is the unsolved, unsolvable wonder.

To Be, in its two connections of inward and outward, the mind and nature. The wonder subsists, and age, though of eternity, could not approach a solution. . . . Who are we and what is Nature have one answer in the life that rushes into us.

I believe the mind is the creator of the world, and is ever creating; — that at last Matter is dead Mind; that mind makes the senses it sees with; that the genius of man is a continuation of the power that made him and that has not done making him.

L ife is incessant parturition.

Higher Truth

Above the thought is the higher truth, — truth as yet undomesticated and therefore unformulated.

I dare not deal with this element in its pure essence. It is too rare for the wings of words.

There is in nature a parallel unity which corresponds to the unity in the mind and makes it available . . . . Not only man puts things in a row, but things belong in a row.

Without identity at base, chaos must be forever.

The Key

Therefore our own organization is a perpetual key, and a well–ordered mind brings to the study of every new fact or class of facts a certain divination of that which it shall find.

This reduction to a few laws, to one law, is not a choice of the individual, it is the tyrannical instinct of the mind. There is no solitary flower and no solitary thought.

To be isolated is to be sick, and in so far, dead. The life of the All must stream through us to make the man and the moment great.

If man has organs for breathing, for sight, for locomotion, for taking food, for digesting, for protection by house–building, by attack and defence, for reproduction and love and care of his young, you shall find all the same in the muskrat. There is a perfect correspondence . . . .

If we go through the British Museum or the Jardin des Plantes in Paris, or any cabinet where is some representation of all the kingdoms of nature, we are surprised with occult sympathies; we feel as if looking at our own bone and flesh through coloring and distorting glasses.

From whatever side we look at Nature we seem to be exploring the figure of a disguised man.

Self Reliance

Each man is a new power in Nature. He holds the keys of the world in his hands. No quality in Nature's vast magazines he cannot touch, no truth he cannot see. Silent, passive, even sulkily Nature offers every morning her wealth to man. She is immensely rich; he is welcome to her entire goods, but she speaks no word, will not so much as beckon or cough; only this, she is careful to leave all her doors ajar. . . . In her hundred–gated Thebes every chamber is a new door.

There are two mischievous superstitions, I know not which does the most harm, one, that "I am wiser than you," and the other that "You are wiser than I." The truth is that every man is furnished, if he will heed it, with wisdom necessary to steer his own boat, — if he will not look away from his own to see how his neighbor steers his.

Echo the leaders and they will fast enough see that you have nothing for them. They came to you for something they had not.

Every man is a new method and distributes things anew. If he could attain full size he would take up, first or last, atom by atom, all the world into a new form.

Instinct and Inspiration

In reckoning the sources of our mental power it were fatal to omit that one which pours all the others into its mould; — that unknown country in which all the rivers of our knowledge have their fountains, and which, by its qualities and structure, determines both the nature of the waters and the direction in which they flow.

The healthy mind lies parallel to the currents of nature and sees things in place, or makes discoveries.

Ask what the Instinct declares, and we have little to say. He is no newsmonger, no disputant, no talker. 'T is a taper, a spark in the great night. Yet a spark at which all the illuminations of human arts and sciences were kindled. This is that glimpse of inextinguishable light by which men are guided; though it does not show objects, yet it shows the way.

Instinct is a shapeless giant in the cave, massive, without hands or fingers or articulating lips or teeth or tongue; Behemoth, disdaining speech, disdaining particulars, lurking, surly, invincible, disdaining thoughts, always whole, never distributed, aboriginal, old as nature, and saying, like poor Topsy, "never was born; growed." Indifferent to the dignity of its function, it plays the god in animal nature as in human or as in the angelic, and spends its omniscience on the lowest wants.

This is Instinct, and Inspiration is only this power excited, breaking its silence; the spark bursting into flame.

At a moment in our history the mind's eye opens and we become aware of spiritual facts, of rights, of duties, of thoughts, — a thousand faces of one essence. We call the essence Truth; the particular aspects of it we call thoughts. These facts, this essence, are not new; they are old and eternal, but our seeing of them is new. Having seen them we are no longer brute lumps whirled by Fate, but we pass into the council–chamber and government of nature. In so far as we see them we share their life and sovereignty.

Intellect
and
Perception

This is the first property of the Intellect I am to point out; the mind detaches. A man is intellectual in proportion as he can make an object of every sensation, perception and intuition . . . .

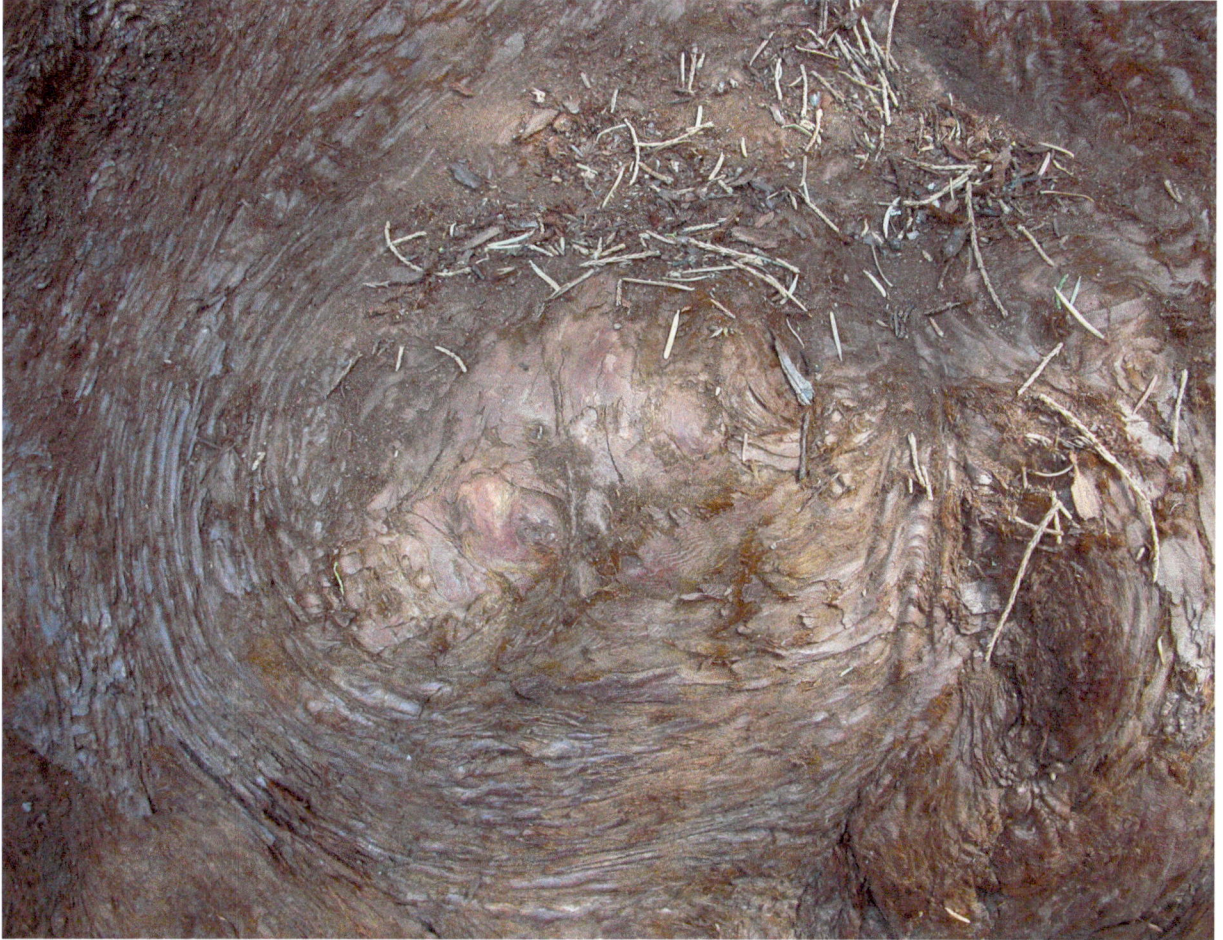

A man of talent has only to name any form or fact with which we are most familiar, and the strong light which he throws on it enhances it to all eyes. People wonder they never saw it before. The detachment consists in seeing it under a new order, not under a personal but under a universal light. To us it had economic, but to the universe it has poetic relations, and it is as good as sun and star now.

A perception is always a generalization. It lifts the object, whether in material or moral nature, into a type. The animal, the low degrees of intellect, know only individuals. The philosopher knows only laws.

Insight assimilates the thing seen. Is it only another way of affirming and illustrating this to say that it sees nothing alone, but sees each particular object in just connections, — sees all in God?

A single thought has no limit to its value; a thought, properly speaking, — that is a truth held not from any man's saying so, or any accidental benefit or recommendation it has in our trade or circumstance, but because we have perceived it is a fact in the nature of things, and in all times and places will and must be the same thing, — is of inestimable value.

A perception, it is of a necessity older than the sun and moon, and the Father of the Gods.

D o not trifle with your perceptions, or hold them cheap. They are your door to the seven heavens . . . .

Genius

The universe is traversed by paths or bridges or stepping-stones across the gulfs of space in every direction. To every soul that is created is its path, invisible to all but itself.

Genius is a delicate sensibility to the laws of the world, adding the power to express them again in some new form.

I owe to genius always the same debt, of lifting the curtain from the common and showing me that gods are sitting disguised in every company.

My measure for all subjects of science as of events is their impression on the soul. . . .There are times when the cawing of a crow, a weed, a snow–flake, a boy's willow whistle, or a farmer planting in his field is more suggestive to the mind than the Yosemite gorge or the Vatican would be in another hour.

But sensibility does not exhaust our idea of it. That is only half. Genius is not a lazy angel contemplating itself and things. It is insatiable for expression. Thought must take the stupendous step of passing into realization. A master can formulate his thought. Our thoughts at first possess us. Later, if we have good heads, we come to possess them.

Will

Will is always miraculous, being the presence of God to men.

There is a meter which determines the constructive power of man, — this, namely, the question whether the mind possesses the control of its thoughts, or they of it. The new sect stands for certain thoughts. We go to individual members for an exposition of them. Vain expectation. They are possessed by the ideas but do not possess them.

107

Shakespeare astonishes by his equality in every play, act, scene or line. One would say he must have been a thousand years old when he wrote his first line, so thoroughly is his thought familiar to him, and has such scope and so solidly worded, as if it were already a proverb and not hereafter to become one.

The secret of power, intellectual or physical, is concentration, and all concentration involves of necessity a certain narrowness. . . . If you ask what compensation is made for the inevitable narrowness, why, this, that in learning one thing well you learn all things.

I must think we are entitled to powers far transcending any that we possess; that we have in the race the sketch of a man which no individual comes up to.

Every sincere man is right, or, to make him right, only needs a little larger dose of his own personality.

The tree or the brook has no duplicity, no pretentiousness, no show. It is, with all its might and main, what it is, and makes one and the same impression and effect at all times.

The daily history of the Intellect is this alternating of expansions and concentrations. The expansions are the invitations from heaven to try a larger sweep, a higher pitch than we have yet climbed, and to leave all our past for this enlarged scope.

No wonder the children love masks and costumes, and play horse, play soldier, play school, play bear, and delight in theatricals. The children have only the instinct of the universe, in which becoming somewhat else is the perpetual game of nature, and death the penalty of standing still. 'T is not less in thought.

Inspiration is the continuation of the divine effort that built the man. The same course continues itself in the mind which we have witnessed in nature . . . .

So long as you are capable of advance, so long you have not abdicated the hope and future of a divine soul.

Love

The spiritual power of man is twofold, mind and heart, Intellect and morals; one respecting truth, the other the will. . . . One is power, the other is love.

If the first rule is to obey your genius, in the second place the good mind is known by the choice of what is positive, of what is advancing. We must embrace the affirmative. But the affirmative of affirmatives is love.

The measure of mental health is the disposition to find good everywhere, good and order, analogy, health and benefit, — the love of truth, tendency to be in the right, no fighter for victory, no cockerel.

We have all of us by nature a certain divination and parturient vaticination in our minds of some higher good and perfection than either power or knowledge.

One

A ristotle declares that the origin of reason is not reason but something better.

The height of culture, the highest behavior, consists in the identification of the Ego with the universe; so that when a man says I hope, I find, I think, he might properly say, The human race thinks or finds or hopes.

I may well say this is divine, the continuation of the divine effort. Alas! it seems not to be ours, to be quite independent of us. Often there is so little affinity between the man and his works that we think the wind must have writ them.

The superiority of the man is in the simplicity of his thought, that he has no obstruction, but looks straight at the pure fact, with no color of option. Profound sincerity is the only basis of talent as of character. The virtue of the Intellect is its own, its courage is of its own kind, and at last it will be justified, though for the moment it seem hostile to what it most reveres.

We wish to sum up the conflicting impressions by saying that all point at last to a unity which inspires all. Our poetry, our religion are its skirts and penumbrae. Yet the charm of life is the hints we derive from this. They overcome us like perfumes from a far–off shore of sweetness, and their meaning is that no tongue shall syllable it without leave; that only itself can name it; that by casting ourselves on it and being its voice it rushes each moment to positive commands, creating men and methods, and ties the will of a child to the love of the First Cause.

Commentary

Mind

p. 4 – I believe in the existence of the material world as the expression of the spiritual or the real, and in the impenetrable mystery which hides (and hides through absolute transparency) the mental nature . . . .

This is the heart of the matter: that the material world is not the Real, and that the Real is connected with our mental nature through a mystery that is both transparent and impenetrable. Emerson's task is to make the transparent at least translucent so that we can see the glass, and not merely through it. He offers us the chance to see what eludes us, the immanent presence of the transcendent that is most akin to our mental nature, and because of this similarity is expressed to us as the material world. We will go with Emerson on this journey, and if at the end we find only ourselves, perhaps by then we will not be surprised.

p. 6 – Every object in nature is a word to signify some fact in the mind. But when that fact is not yet put into English words, when I look at the tree or the river and have not yet definitely made out what they would say to me, they are by no means unimpressive. I wait for them, I enjoy them before they yet speak. I feel as if I stood by an ambassador charged with the message of his king, which he does not deliver because the hour when he should say it is not yet arrived.

The great question of Nature has always faced mankind, whether it was called by this name, or by any name. If, with Buber,[1] we divide the world into "Thou" and "It," we still must leave room for that unfathomable "I" that stands in opposition (It) or relationship (Thou) to the other. The question of Nature speaks to the distinctness of this "I" for it asks of its boundaries, or if it is separate at all. Surrounded as we are by the man–molded world of things, we separate ourselves from that which would speak so that even our bodies become "It," and mute. Even my body, as Nature, poses this question. Is that tumor, I? Can I even control that which seems to be most intimately part of myself, my body?

p. 8 – Whilst we converse with truths as thoughts, they exist also as plastic forces; as the soul of a man, the soul of a plant, the genius or constitution of any part of nature, which makes it what it is. The thought which was in the world, part and parcel of the world, has disengaged itself and taken an independent existence.

If we are to transform the world of things, to hear their voices as did Adam, we must allow them to speak again from that old fire that we have quenched with externality. As long as they are "they" (even if that "they" be "Thou"), they will at most whisper — unquiet voices kept low so as not to disturb.

p. 10– I wish to know the laws of this wonderful power, that I may domesticate it. I observe with curiosity its risings and settings, illumination and eclipse; its obstructions and its provocations, that I may learn to live with it wisely, court its aid, catch sight of its splendor, feel its approach, hear and save its oracles and obey them.

It is not their voices that are low, but our talk that is loud. It drowns their voices to obscurity with its undomesticated chatter. It is not idle chance that our landfills overflow with garbage.

p. 12 – In my thought I seem to stand on the bank of a river and watch the endless flow of the stream, floating objects of all shapes, colors and natures; nor can I much detain them as they pass, except by running beside them a little way along the bank. But whence they come or whither they go is not told me. Only I have a suspicion that, as geologists say every river makes its own valley, so does this mystic stream. It makes its valley, makes its banks and makes perhaps the observer too.

That which we value, we create. The love of ease, of gratification, chokes us with its sufficiency. The thing is more important than the means; and so we drown in ugliness, our souls crying for beauty. — It is more important to eat than to enjoy; to arrive than travel; to have than to . . . but there is nothing more important than to have, and to have more.[2] What is created by this sufficiency, and more than sufficiency?

p. 14 – Who has found the boundaries of human intelligence? Who has made a chart of its channel or approached the fountain of this wonderful Nile?

A giant Sequoia may live 3,000 years before it dies of age, lightning, and fire. And yet in this instant those ages can be encompassed and assimilated. They exist NOW; are understood NOW, are experienced NOW. All past, all future, is held NOW in the boundless human intelligence. There is nowhere else it could be. Nowhere else that it is.

Being

p. 18. – To Be is the unsolved, unsolvable wonder.

All being exits in that unfathomable slice of

time that is NOW, and like Leibnitz's[3] monads[4] reflects all other being — lives in and as part of that being.

p. 20 – *To Be, in its two connections of inward and outward, the mind and nature. The wonder subsists, and age, though of eternity, could not approach a solution. . . . Who are we and what is Nature have one answer in the life that rushes into us.*

We must remember that when Emerson says "being" he does not mean that world of things that is taken so often for the Real. Our creations mislead us in this regard. They make us think that all nature is dead and should be subject to our will; and because we think this, we make it so.

p. 22 – *I believe the mind is the creator of the world, and is ever creating; — that at last Matter is dead Mind; that mind makes the senses it sees with; that the genius of man is a continuation of the power that made him and that has not done making him.*

There is a circle here, and a mystery. My body is matter and external. My brain is part of my body, and external — an object among objects. Can my brain then think, and recognize itself? Nietzsche[5] shows the fallacy of this argument. He asks "Is the world the creation of the senses?"

Then the eye must be such a creation. Can the eye be a creation of the eye? "Whatever the world is, it is NOT the creation of the senses." Whatever thought is, it is NOT the creation of the brain.

p. 24 – *Life is incessant parturition.*

If thought is not the creation of the brain, what can it be? To live with the tension this question provokes, moment by moment, is to be born anew — in this moment, in every moment. Live with it, and watch the world change.

Higher Truth

p. 28 – *Above the thought is the higher truth, — truth as yet undomesticated and therefore unformulated.*

Silent, without words there lives that of which thought is the poor step–child. The mother of thought, the great waters. Silent . . . Immense . . . Luminous.

p. 30 – *I dare not deal with this element in its pure essence. It is too rare for the wings of words.*

The tao that can be told
is not the eternal Tao.

The name that can be named
is not the eternal Name.

The unnameable
is the eternally real.
Naming is the origin
of all particular things."[6]

p. 32 – There is in nature a parallel unity which corresponds to the unity in the mind and makes it available. . . . Not only man puts things in a row, but things belong in a row.

Whence comes the unreasonable effectiveness of mathematics?[7] How is it that a pure creation of the mind has any relationship to the external world, let alone a relationship that is accurate to ten decimal places?

p. 34 – Without identity at base, chaos must be forever.

If our thoughts could not access the unity that dwells in things, not only would mathematics fail, but nothing of the sense world would have any meaning for us. The world comes to us from two sides: thought and sense, but a unity underlies it all.[8]

The most incomprehesible thing about
the universe is that it is comprehensible.
— Albert Einstein

The Key

p. 38 – Therefore our own organization is a perpetual key, and a well–ordered mind brings to the study of every new fact or class of facts a certain divination of that which it shall find.

This is the hardest part: seeing that we ourselves are the key. The idea that the human being is a microcosm of macrocosmic creation is one form in which this has traditionally been expressed. Let us take typical refutation of this idea and see where it leads.

By natural teleology is meant the idea
that all changes in nature are made for
a purpose. But the only purposes we
know anything about are human purposes. . . . The projection of human
rhythms into the cosmos is only one
form of identifying the microcosm and
the macrocosm.[9]

Following this line of thought we conclude
that the correspondence between the human

154

organization and nature is false, a projection of human purposes. Nature exists outside of, and apart from, us. Any other view mistakes inner processes for external ones.

Let us look at this argument more closely. Let us turn it around. We see a process in nature and describe it as external, and apart from us. We see this process as having no purpose in relationship to us. "But the only purposes we know anything about are human purposes." This includes the purpose of having no purpose. We only know that something has no purpose because we assign it that function. Just as the projection of human rhythms into the cosmos involves a human decision making process, the process of seeing something as external, of denying a connection between ourselves and other aspects of the world, is a human process. In both cases we see the world as a projection of an aspect of our being.

We have tried to escape ourselves, but have failed. What we normally think of as the external world, is internal. The world is in us. Even our bodies are internal. We look for the outer world, but cannot find it.

Try this if you want a more visceral demonstration. Locate any object, then point to it. It is "there." But what is it that is pointing? You? Your finger! Where is your finger? In the external world? Point now at your pointing finger. Then at the finger pointing at the pointing finger. Use your nose. Then point at your nose. What is left to point with? Your eye? Do it; then point at it. Point at your eye. — Eventually the game ends. There is nothing left to point with. Where is that thing that forms the final resting place from which you point? Do you find it in the external world? If so, point at it and begin again. You come at last to the interior I. Aware of the world in thought, it finds the word in itself and calls it "external." This externality is a myth, the myth of the modern age. The external as external exists only to the extent that we think it does. In the future we will find in us what we now see outside of us, on all levels.

p. 40 – This reduction to a few laws, to one law, is not a choice of the individual, it is the tyrannical instinct of the mind. There is no solitary flower and no solitary thought.

The human being is the one law. We are the unity that contains the seeming multiplicity of things, and of thought. This is not a choice. We cannot escape ourselves, though we try incessantly. Those who have thought it through see this. "It is the tyrannical instinct of the mind."

p. 42 – To be isolated is to be sick, and in so far, dead.

The life of the All must stream through us to make the man and the moment great.

Are we not sick today? Isolated in an exterior world, a world we have made but is not ours. Condemned to a life of exteriority; trees to be cut; rivers to be damned; nature to be subdued. What is there that could flow into us? — But learn to open yourself to nature and a new boundless world arises within you. A world whose only limits are those you set.[10]

p. 44 – If man has organs for breathing, for sight, for locomotion, for taking food, for digesting, for protection by house–building, by attack and defence, for reproduction and love and care of his young, you shall find all the same in the muskrat. There is a perfect correspondence. . . .

We look into the world, and find ourselves. The correspondence in structure has long been known, and been explained in various ways: divine creation, evolution from a common ancestor. Whatever explanation we accept, the correspondence remains. It is not affected by our explanations.

p. 46 – If we go through the British Museum or the Jardin des Plantes in Paris, or any cabinet where is some representation of all the kingdoms of nature, we are surprised with occult sympathies; we feel as if looking at our own bone and flesh through coloring and distorting glasses.

It is our own flesh, and it looks back at us. It is startling in its seeming alienness, and frightening.

p. 48 – From whatever side we look at Nature we seem to be exploring the figure of a disguised man.

The resemblance is not superficial. If confronted with your kidney, would you recognize it as you?

Self Reliance

p. 52 – Each man is a new power in Nature. He holds the keys of the world in his hands. No quality in Nature's vast magazines he cannot touch, no truth he cannot see. Silent, passive, even sulkily Nature offers every morning her wealth to man. She is immensely rich; he is welcome to her entire goods, but she speaks no word, will not so much as beckon or cough; only this, she is careful to leave all her doors ajar. . . . In her hundred–gated Thebes every chamber is a new door.

Each human being, a New Power? — Just because the world is in us does not mean that it is fully known. Much remains unknown, unconscious. Who is enough himself or herself to face this unknown, to open the doors?

p. 54 – There are two mischievous superstitions, I know not which does the most harm, one, that "I am wiser than you," and the other that "You are wiser than I." The truth is that every man is furnished, if he will heed it, with wisdom necessary to steer his own boat, — if he will not look away from his own to see how his neighbor steers his.

Ask a Buddhist how to govern your life. He will tell you what is valuable to him. Ask a Christian why you should believe in Christ. She will tell you why she believes. Ask a Hindu about Krishna. He will tell you what has given his life meaning. Where can you find meaning in your life, if not in yourself?

For I have come to the conclusion, in my own experience, that those who, no matter to what faith they belong, reverently study the teachings of other faiths, broaden their own instead of narrowing their hearts.
— Mahatma Gandhi

p. 56 – Echo the leaders and they will fast enough see that you have nothing for them. They came to you for something they had not.

These leaders are not the "leaders" of sycophants. Those leaders demand adoration. Emerson speaks of the leaders who blaze new ground; who make the unconscious conscious; who open doors. They want what you bring of yourself because it enriches what they have. They do not fear the unknown.

p. 58 – Every man is a new method and distributes things anew. If he could attain full size he would take up, first or last, atom by atom, all the world into a new form.

Emerson's fame comes from this, that he grew larger than most and left the world changed.

Instinct and Inspiration

p. 62 – In reckoning the sources of our mental power it were fatal to omit that one which pours all the others into its mould; — that unknown country in which all the rivers of our knowledge have their fountains, and which, by its qualities and structure, determines both the nature of the waters and the direction in which they flow.

Let us follow Nietzsche's lead and try to find the source of the world. Perhaps then we will understand that "unknown country" of which Emerson speaks.

We know that the visible world cannot be the product of the senses, for the senses cannot be a product of themselves. Does it lie in the objects themselves? Is the world "objective," composed of objects? When we follow any quality of an object to its source we come back to ourselves. What we see as color, as form, as location, can all be traced to our senses and mind. Color blindness is a simple example of this. Those with the most common form of red–green color blindness (deuteranomaly) see less green than a "normally sighted" person. Relative to "normal" their sight is green weak. For them, a full pallet of colors consists of red and blue. Since full pallet mixtures are seen as white (red, green and blue mixtures are white to people with "normal" color vision), deuteranope's see mixtures of red and blue (i.e., purple) as white. About 5% of men and 0.35% of women have this type of color blindness. Because the majority of people see "full" greens as well as reds and blues, we consider this condition normal and attribute to the object the possesion of the "full" color spectrum seen by those with normal color vision. In truth, the qualities possessed by the object are just as much a creation of our senses (and mind) as of the object itself. If we were all deuteranopes, there would be no purple

The phenomenon of synesthesia demonstrates this even more clearly. Those with synesthesia experience a joining of the senses so that the synesthete may hear colors, or taste shapes. To a synesthete the world is a rich and rewarding place, full of wonder.[11] Melodies have shapes and numbers have color. The existence of synesthesia reinforces the fact that the qualities of objects do not reside in the objects themselves. The same object seen by different observers has different qualities. This fact even extends to the perception of shape and extension,[12] qualities which Locke[13] took to be the primary, measurable, objective aspects of external reality. These considerations show us that we cannot find the world in the objects that we perceive. Does it then lie in the atoms?

The world does not lie in the atoms. The atom is a conceptual model used to summarize a great number of experiments and experiences, obtained both through the senses and with the aid of instruments.[14] If we endow the atom with sensory qualities, it is because we learned to visualize it from diagrams intended to simplify the underlying experiments and mathematical formulations. Although we often project the qualities we assign to atoms into the external world, it is important to realize that these qualities are not found there. A model cannot be the basis for the world that we are seeking.

We have sought the basis of the world, and found nothing. The source of our mental power must be found within that power itself, not in the "external world." Our thought is the harbinger of that which flows from that unknown country of which Emerson speaks.

p. 64 – The healthy mind lies parallel to the currents of nature and sees things in place, or makes discoveries.

Right thought comes spontaneously, comes like the morning wind; comes daily, like our daily bread, to humble service; comes duly to those who look for it. It does not need to pump your brains and force thought to think rightly.

— Emerson (NHI)

p. 66 – Ask what the Instinct declares, and we have little to say. He is no newsmonger, no disputant, no talker. 'T is a taper, a spark in the great night. Yet a spark at which all the illuminations of human arts and sciences were kindled. This is that glimpse of inextinguishable light by which men are guided; though it does not show objects, yet it shows the way.

Instinct is that power by which we find, without conscious reflection, what is Right.

p. 68– Instinct is a shapeless giant in the cave, massive, without hands or fingers or articulating lips or teeth or tongue; Behemoth, disdaining speech, disdaining particulars, lurking, surly, invincible, disdaining thoughts, always whole, never distributed, aboriginal, old as nature, and saying, like poor Topsy, "never was born; growed." Indifferent to the dignity of its function, it plays the god in animal nature as in human or as in the angelic, and spends its omniscience on the lowest wants.

How does a colt know how to stand the moment it is born; a stickleback fish to build a mating burrow and nest that is just shorter than its body length; a honey bee to make perfect, six–sided cells; a human infant to suckle? A psychologist will tell you that these behaviors are inherited, and contrast them with learned behavior. But this is no explanation. It merely pushes the question back to a level where we have no direct experience, the level of the gene. How do genes code for behavior? How are they activated at precisely the correct time? When we know the answers to these questions we will still be left with the raw phenomena, which mechanisms can never explain.

p. 70 – This is Instinct, and Inspiration is only this power excited, breaking its silence; the spark bursting into flame.

Inspiration is that power by which we find, with reflection, but not dependent upon it, what is Right.

p. 72 – At a moment in our history the mind's eye opens and we become aware of spiritual facts, of rights, of duties, of thoughts, — a thousand faces of one essence. We call the essence Truth; the particular aspects of it we call thoughts. These facts, this essence, are not new; they are old and eternal, but our seeing of them is new. Having seen them we are no longer brute lumps whirled by Fate, but we pass into the council–chamber and government of nature. In so far as we see them we share their life and sovereignty.

A thought is not the Truth. No thought can be. At most it points toward that unknown country that quickens us to share its "life and sovereignty."

Intellect and Perception

p. 76 – This is the first property of the Intellect I am to point out; the mind detaches. A man is intellectual in proportion as he can make an object of every sensa-tion, perception and intuition . . . .

The world consists of discrete objects because of this property of the intellect. Through the intellect we detach things from their context, and then project them into the sensory world as objects. There is nothing in the things that requires that they be seen as objects. We could, and sometimes do, see them in their context. Mystics call this the experience of oneness. Kant[15] called the power to detach "intellect" and contrasted it with the synthetic power of reason. The intellect sees distinction, reason, unity. In more contemporary language we might call these modes of thought analytic and holistic,[16] and relate them to research in cognitive psychology.[17] Analytic perception is the propensity to view an object as composed of parts, to focus on the parts in opposition to the whole. Holistic perception is the propensity to see the whole in contrast to the parts. The technical definition of holistic perception is even more surprising. Holistic perception is the inability to focus on a part of an object even when specifically instructed to do so. That human beings possess this capacity has been shown experimentally.

p. 78 – A man of talent has only to name any form or fact with which we are most familiar, and the strong light which he throws on it enhances it to all eyes. People wonder they never saw it before. The detachment consists in seeing it under a new order, not under a personal but under a universal light. To us it had economic, but to the universe it has poetic relations, and it is as good as sun and star now.

The Sea

Incorrigible, ruthless,
It rattled the shingly beach of my childhood,
Subtle, the opposite of earth,
And unlike earth, capable
Any time at all of proclaiming eternity
Like something or someone to whom
We have to surrender, finding
Through that surrender life.

— Louis MacNeice[18]

p. 80 – A perception is always a generalization. It lifts the object, whether in material or moral nature, into a type. The animal, the low degrees of intellect, know only individuals. The philosopher knows only laws.

We should not seek for this definition of perception in a textbook or dictionary. It is Emerson's own. In perception we "see" an object. We combine sensory stimulus and thought so that the object becomes less inert, and more real. All people make this combination. We would not recognize that oddly rectangular object with "leaves" as a book if we did not. The recognition of the object creates the object in our experience. It did not exist for us as that object before we recognized it. — Think of a time when you could not identify something; a vaguely distinguishable object low in the sky, perhaps. It only became the moon seen through clouds when you linked this concept with what your senses revealed. It could have been, and was, anything. Perhaps you played a guessing game with yourself before your recognized it: water tower, plane, flying saucer (!) — For the man or woman who values their intellect, for the philosopher, these links are rich with meaning. They lift the object from its mundane relations to those that have universal importance.

p. 82 – Insight assimilates the thing seen. Is it only another way of affirming and illustrating this to say that it sees nothing alone, but sees each particular object in just connections, — sees all in God?

That which is seen is not external. The act of seeing is something that takes place inside of us. What we see is a part of us. All perception is an internal act. We say "I see what exists," but when we look for the object we find only more acts of perception. Where do we find that object that exists prior to our perception of it? How would we know it if we found it? There is no object that exists in itself, alone, apart from our perception of it. If there were, we could have no knowledge of it, and thus for us it would not exist. It is a small step from "I perceive it" to "it exists." Perception, not existence, comes first. This seems counterintuitive only because we have the habit of thinking otherwise. We think "I perceive an object because it exists," when in fact we know it exists because we perceive it. Objects do not have an existence that is external to us. Each object is related, through us, to all other objects and thoughts.

The spatial relations "beside," "upon," "near," and so on, are only one type of relationship between objects. These relationships are not primary, but are special in that they are easy for others to verify. Other types of relationships may be less easy to verify, but are as real. Looking at the cup sitting before me, I may estimate the thermal conductivity of the ceramic. This conductivity is as rightly associated with the cup as is the concept "It sits on my desk."

p. 84 – A single thought has no limit to its value; a thought, properly speaking, — that is a truth held not from any man's saying so, or any accidental benefit or recommendation it has in our trade or circumstance, but because we have perceived it is a fact in the nature of things, and in all times and places will and must be the same thing, — is of inestimable value.

Are not all thoughts like this? Are not all thoughts true in and of themselves, not because any person says that they are? It is this quality of thought that gives it its value. All thoughts are true. It is only if we insist on a strict representational role for language that we run into problems. If we insist that Lloyd George[19] must be alive, in London, and asleep at this moment for the phrase "Lloyd George is sleeping in London" to be true, then we will have difficulty with the idea that all thoughts are true. Emerson's claim goes to a deeper level. It does not depend on any specific reference, but on the <u>ability</u> of thought, and thus language, to act in a referential way. It is not important that at this moment Lloyd George is <u>not</u> alive and is <u>not</u> sleeping in London, but that there was, or at least could be, a time when Lloyd George was asleep in London. This thought bears the type of truth of which Emerson speaks because it has the capability to refer to a condition of the world in which Lloyd George is asleep in London. When you reflect on it, this is a truly amazing property of thought. We take it for granted, but there is no reason that our thought should be like this. Our thoughts could have no relationship to our world of experience. In fact, there are people whose thought is like this, having

162

no, or at best a distorted relationship to the world that most of us experience. Schizophrenics[20] are perhaps the most obvious example of this phenomenon.

From these considerations, we see that we can divide the property of thoughts into two classes. There are those properties that emerge when a specific thought or chain of thoughts has a direct connection with our experience of an event in the world. This is not the property that Emerson is referring to when he speaks of the truth of a thought. The other property of thoughts is their ability to reference events in the world, whether those events are true in the first sense or not. This is the deeper meaning of the truth of thought. It is the intensive, inner meaning of the phrase. Without this quality, there would be no possibility of thought being true in the first sense.

p. 86 – A perception, it is of a necessity older than the sun and moon, and the Father of the Gods.

It is significant that Emerson says "is of a necessity." We should not ignore this phrase, or trivialize its meaning. The sun, the moon, and the Father of the Gods are all concepts. We may link these concepts with sensations; they may have been stimulated by sensations; but they are NOT pre–existing, pre–defined, external objects that force themselves on our senses. We create them in the act of perception, in the act of uniting sensory or mental stimuli with thought. The process of perception must come first. There is no other choice.

p. 88 – Do not trifle with your perceptions, or hold them cheap. They are your door to the seven heavens . . . .

Because the process of perception must come first, our perceptions are the key to all aspects of the world, to the "seven heavens." If this seems counterintuitive, perhaps it is because our perceptions are so abundant. We are tempted to hold them cheap because we are given them in excess. When we think of that which is rare as valuable, we are using the same mode of thought as when dealing with objects in the sense world. Platinum is valuable because it is very rare. In the spiritual world it is not that which is rare that is valuable, but that which is abundant. In the spiritual world we are faced with the problem of maintaining our sense of self in the face of overwhelming abundance. The problem is learning to accept this abundance, abundance that seems as if it would drown us. Our perceptions of the visible world are just the outer threshold of this abundance. The abundance of the spirit, which begins with our thoughts, is by comparison a Niagara.

Genius

p. 92 – The universe is traversed by paths or bridges or stepping-stones across the gulfs of space in every direction. To every soul that is created is its path, invisible to all but itself.

How are we to find our way within this abundance? Is not each day in which we wake to find ourselves a day of magic, when miracles happen? The path that I find through the day, and which binds me to myself day after day, is one that not only is, but only can be visible to myself, and then perhaps only at the end of my life when, looking back, I see the pattern that has been created for me by my daily actions. What is right for me is not right for you or for any other soul. I must find my path even if at times I do so blindly. To do otherwise, to follow or to try to follow someone else's path, can only lead to unhappiness and disappointment.

p. 94 – Genius is a delicate sensibility to the laws of the world, adding the power to express them again in some new form.

Finding one's path in the world requires ge-

nius, is genius expressed. The new form in which the laws are expressed need not be the form of some external object or theory, but may be the form of your own life. In finding your path you find yourself; you create yourself. The artist does this in creating an object, a part of him or herself. But we are all artists. Our canvas is our flesh and bone. To find happiness, our creation must fit the laws of the world, and for this we need the delicate sensibility of which Emerson speaks. If we are not sensitive to it, we will try to travel against the current. This can only lead to misery.

p. 96 – I owe to genius always the same debt, of lifting the curtain from the common and showing me that gods are sitting disguised in every company.

The gods are with us along our path at every step, though we may not always perceive them.

p. 98 – My measure for all subjects of science as of events is their impression on the soul. . . . There are times when the cawing of a crow, a weed, a snow-flake, a boy's willow whistle, or a farmer planting in his field is more suggestive to the mind than the Yosemite gorge or the Vatican would be in another hour.

When the things of the world or the subjects of the intellect impress us, it is because we see through them and obtain a glimpse of the unknown country that lies behind all perceptions. That one thing impresses us now and another later is about the things, yes, but ever more is about us. We see what we are ready for, what we have prepared ourselves to see. Those who have done little preparation, see little. Those who have done much, see much.

p. 100 – But sensibility does not exhaust our idea of it. That is only half. Genius is not a lazy angel contemplating itself and things. It is insatiable for expression. Thought must take the stupendous step of passing into realization. A master can formulate his thought. Our thoughts at first possess us. Later, if we have good heads, we come to possess them.

The final and most true realization of thought is not a thing, but life itself. Ultimately, it will be our own life, but on the way to that ultimate and unifying end, we shape the lives of others. We are not islands isolated in the stream of life. What I do, what I feel, is connected to what you do, what you feel; what you do, what you feel, is connected to me; and so on through all the generations of man and woman. Even the past is not separate. It lives in each of us — is realized in each of us — first as thought, later as action, and ultimately as part of our all-connected selves.

Will

p. 104 – Will is always miraculous, being the presence of God to men.

Our actions affect all things, all life. When we do anything, the world is changed. Every action, as it leaves us, becomes less of us and more of the world. Our actions are no longer ours when they are done. We will reclaim them in the end, when we realize the unity that is implicit in our natures, but until then, they are part of the world. Their origin comes through us, born on the angel-wings of will.

p. 106 – There is a meter which determines the constructive power of man, — this, namely, the question whether the mind possesses the control of its thoughts, or they of it. The new sect stands for certain thoughts. We go to individual members for an exposition of them. Vain expectation. They are possessed by the ideas but do not possess them.

That which enters the world through our actions may be for good, or ill. Those acts that are constructive, anabolic, come out of who we are in the deepest sense. Those that are destructive, catabolic, come through us in acts of possession. Think of the adoration which Hitler received when he entered Austria during the Anschluss,[21] or the atrocities of Kristallnacht.[22] Were not these people possessed, as we can all be possessed by an idea we have not mastered? The worst can happen only when we are possessed. Then we think that the world must be, SO (!). There can be no doubt, for if we doubt even one thing, we doubt all. Thus think those possessed. How different this is from our inner world when we possess our thoughts. Then we do not fear to turn them to every corner so that we may better understand that which we have mastered. We, not they, control the interaction.

p. 108 – Shakespeare astonishes by his equality in every play, act, scene or line. One would say he must have been a thousand years old when he wrote his first line, so thoroughly is his thought familiar to him, and has such scope and so solidly worded, as if it were already a proverb and not hereafter to become one.

Where can we look for guidance in mastering our thought? Emerson points to Shakespeare not as an idol, but as an example of one who has reached the peak of human performance. All those who have reached this peak can serve us if we are able to find ourselves in their shoes. When their performance is extraordinary it is difficult to believe that we can each accomplish something similar. At times like these we must remember that what one has done, all of us have done. As Shakespeare wrote, so do we all. Our accomplishment may not be in literature, but is no less for that. Excellence in any endeavor requires self–mastery, which is largely mastery of our mental life, of our thought. The problem is only one of belief. We must not believe that we each bear the seeds of greatness, we must <u>know</u> it. Then we can begin to cultivate the germ of greatness that lies in each one of us.

p. 110 – The secret of power, intellectual or physical, is concentration, and all concentration involves of necessity a certain narrowness. . . . If you ask what compensation is made for the inevitable narrowness, why, this, that in learning one thing well you learn all things.

When we do it with intensity, all things are in the one thing we are doing now. When we write, sing, dance, love, paint, teach . . . with intensity, we reach into that unknown country and bring to light something wild and strange; something with the power to change our life, and the lives of others. This discovery requires concentration. It leads to a transformation that has little to do with our subject, and much to do with the best that lies in each of us.

p. 112 – I must think we are entitled to powers far transcending any that we possess; that we have in the race the sketch of a man which no individual comes up to.

In these moments of transcendence we touch that man, that woman, who is only sketched in our daily lives. These moments can become the doorways through which we glimpse our true potential. Through them we learn to transform all of the moments of our lives. We each must do this to and for ourselves, but we do not do it alone. Each one who works to transform him or herself brings us closer to that day when the sketch will be realized in flesh.

p. 114 – Every sincere man is right, or, to make him right, only needs a little larger dose of his own personality.

The sincere man or woman is not possessed. He and she are on the way to discovering the freedom that comes when they are fully themselves. This does not result from a strengthening of their lower, immature, acquisitive egos, but from coming into their own within their True, higher ego, which is intrinsically connected to all other people and things. Our personalities, when developed through our genius, can become so transparent that our True ego can shine through. By becoming more ourselves, we become more of who we are as part of God.

p. 116 – The tree or the brook has no duplicity, no pretentiousness, no show. It is, with all its might and main, what it is, and makes one and the same impression and effect at all times.

How different is this from what the media tells us we should be. The media tell us that we should find happiness in things, in the purchase and possession of things. If we follow this advice, all life becomes show and shallow. We lose the force of ourselves, that force that can make us like a flower, a brook, a tree.

p. 118 – The daily history of the Intellect is this alternating of expansions and concentrations. The expansions are the invitations from heaven to try a larger sweep, a higher pitch than we have yet climbed, and to leave all our past for this enlarged scope.

The contractions would seem to be the hurts, the injustices, the injuries that wound and limit us. But when we meet them with an open heart, saying "yes" to all that comes to us, these are not contractions but the invitations to live life more fully and deeply.[23] There is no event that can wound us once we know this. We can be challenged, but not harmed. Harm comes from contraction, from pulling away, from saying "no." This is when we are vulnerable, when we can be hurt, when we can hurt others. Opening toward the ever–present Yes allows us to expand into the challenge, to see it as it really is: an invitation to leave the past for an enlarged scope.

p. 120 – No wonder the children love masks and costumes, and play horse, play soldier, play school, play bear, and delight in theatricals. The children have only the instinct of the universe, in which becoming somewhat else is the perpetual game of nature, and death the penalty of standing still. 'T is not less in thought.

When we reach for a higher sweep we, like a child, become something else. We leave behind a portion of who we thought we were, and embark on a voyage to discover more of ourself. Like all voyages, this one may seem frightening. The fear is born out of our most primal instinct: the instinct of self–preservation. Who will I be if I am not myself? Who will I be when I give up those qualities by which I define myself? We stand on the edge of an abyss, and look down into what seems to be nothingness. This abyss will be our fate and death unless we find the courage to take a step into the seeming nothingness.

p. 122 – Inspiration is the continuation of the divine effort that built the man. The same course continues itself in the mind which we have witnessed in nature . . . .

The grand scope that built us, calls us, and though the next step seems to be into the abyss, we must take it if we are to remain true to ourselves. We must know that as we step, we will find support. We must be willing to fall so that we can be supported. If we demand to know where each step, where each day, each year, will take us, we die. Death is the only surety of the future. All else seems chaos. To see it as more requires only a step . . . and then another . . . and another. This is an act of breathing, of inspiration; both mental and physical. Mental because we must overcome the lassitude of thought that would keep us rooted to one spot. Physical because we must remember to breathe, and so overcome our fear.

p. 124 – So long as you are capable of advance, so long you have not abdicated the hope and future of a divine soul.

There is a tremendous amount at stake here. Emerson does not invite us out for a casual stroll.

He asks us to discover for ourselves what is at stake: it is our deepest selves, and with us the world. To think that this is a private matter is to make a fundamental mistake about who we are. We may think "Well, if I do not take up this task or if I fail, it really concerns only myself." These thoughts do not come from our higher self, but from those parts of ourselves that want to remain isolated, alone, and in pain. What one does, we all do. When one is in pain, we all suffer. Eventually, everyone will know this from their own experience. For now, we only look forward to the future, and the promise of a divine soul.

Love

p. 128 – The spiritual power of man is twofold, mind and heart, Intellect and morals; one respecting truth, the other the will. . . . One is power, the other is love.

Power and love are two of God's attributes. With Lucifer, the light–bearer, the intellect, he shared power. With Christ, our heart, ourself, he shared love.

p. 130 – If the first rule is to obey your genius, in the second place the good mind is known by the choice of what is positive, of what is advancing. We must embrace the affirmative. But the affirmative of af-

firmatives is love.

These two rules are not separate. To follow your genius is to choose the positive. This is one way you can know we are on the right track: do your choices advance the power of love in you? To know the answer to this question, first find where you have been wounded. If it has been with you for much of your life, it is possible that you define yourself by this wound: I am he or she who suffers because . . . . Find this place, and watch what happens to it as you make life's choices. When your choices affirm love, you will feel its spiritual presence draw near to you. It will not happen all at once, but healing will continue as you learn to embrace the affirmative. You can learn to say yes to everything, even to those events that would previously have been considered hurtful. What you previously considered the greatest ill may bring the deepest blessing. Embracing the affirmative requires that you give up the labels "good" and "bad" and allow things to be what they are. When they are revealed in their true nature, you will see that this nature is love.

p. 132 – The measure of mental health is the disposition to find good everywhere, good and order, analogy, health and benefit, — the love of truth, tendency to be in the right, no fighter for victory, no cockerel.

There is an old German saying "When the cock (cockerel) crows on the dung heap the weather will change . . . or stay the same." There is no need to fight for victory, to proclaim our great place and knowledge — our Truth. Those who do so are like the cock, and equally accurate. What is needed is a "disposition to find good." A disposition that is applied to every situation; a proclivity for approaching the world in a certain way. The proclivity to find good; to attempt it when we can; and when we cannot, or when we fail, to revisit the situation in our minds and redo the interaction, redo the judgment, so that we begin to see the possibility of always turning toward the positive. This is the sign of mental health: to allow the possibility that the situation can be "seen again" in a new and purer light. Without this possibility there will always be the tendency for self–hate. All of our wounds have a bit of this in them. They are linked to times or events in which we have felt, or been made to feel, inadequate. The antidote to these events is to accept them with an open heart.

p. 134 – We have all of us by nature a certain divination and parturient vaticination in our minds of some higher good and perfection than either power or knowledge.

In turning towards the positive, we turn towards our higher selves. That is why we recognize the positive as part of ourselves, as a higher perfection. Imagine it in this way: your higher self stands over you, and each time you choose love it is able to approach you more closely. We feel its presence . . . and its approach is like the coming of spring rain.

One

p. 138 – Aristotle declares that the origin of reason is not reason but something better.

Love and reason seem to be strange bedfellows, but recall how we reached this point. Our wings have been the wings of thought. We have followed Emerson, one of the greatest intellects of his day and found, not a parched landscape, but a verdant forest teaming with life. The path of the intellect only leads to the dry land when it is followed incompletely, or with the wrong intent. The dry land exits, but it is not the destination we find when we follow our genius, when we choose Yes. Yes is not a dry choice. It may not be an easy choice, but it is not dry. Reason, when honestly followed leads inevitably to its source.

p. 140 – The height of culture, the highest behav-

ior, consists in the identification of the Ego with the universe; so that when a man says I hope, I find, I think, he might properly say, The human race thinks or finds or hopes.

Although that unknown source can remain unnamed, it can also now be named. The name is surprising, shocking. The name is "I."

p. 142 – I may well say this is divine, the continuation of the divine effort. Alas! it seems not to be ours, to be quite independent of us. Often there is so little affinity between the man and his works that we think the wind must have writ them.

As Shakespeare wrote; as Einstein thought; as Gandhi lived.

p. 144 – The superiority of the man is in the simplicity of his thought, that he has no obstruction, but looks straight at the pure fact, with no color of option. Profound sincerity is the only basis of talent as of character. The virtue of the Intellect is its own, its courage is of its own kind, and at last it will be justified, though for the moment it seem hostile to what it most reveres.

The virtue of the Intellect is love. It is its own, though this seems impossible. The Intellect and love seem to be inimical to each other until we follow Emerson's path. In the end, which begins now, they will be reconciled, and the powers of the Intellect will be justified.

p. 146 – We wish to sum up the conflicting impressions by saying that all point at last to a unity which inspires all. Our poetry, our religion are its skirts and penumbrae. Yet the charm of life is the hints we derive from this. They overcome us like perfumes from a far–off shore of sweetness, and their meaning is that no tongue shall syllable it without leave; that only itself can name it; that by casting ourselves on it and being its voice it rushes each moment to positive commands, creating men and methods, and ties the will of a child to the love of the First Cause.

To those who have begun to see what lies hidden in the small word "I," I can offer no more significant words than these: The Christ is seeing us.[24]

Natural History of Intellect

Ralph Waldo Emerson

I have used such opportunity as I have had, and lately in London and Paris, to attend scientific lectures; and in listening to Richard Owen's[25] masterly enumeration of the parts and laws of the human body, or Michael Faraday's explanation of magnetic powers, or the botanist's descriptions, one could not help admiring the irresponsible security and happiness of the attitude of the naturalist; sure of admiration for his facts, sure of their sufficiency. They ought to interest you; if they do not, the fault lies with you.

Then I thought — could not a similar enumeration be made of the laws and powers of the Intellect, and possess the same claims on the student? Could we have, that is, the exhaustive accuracy of distribution which chemists use in their nomenclature and anatomists in their descriptions, applied to a higher class of facts; to those laws, namely, which are common to chemistry, anatomy, astronomy geometry, intellect, morals, and social life; — laws of the world?

Why not? These powers and laws are also facts in a Natural History. They also are objects of science, and may be numbered and recorded, like stamens and vertebrae. At the same time they have a deeper interest, as in the order of nature they lie higher and are nearer to the mysterious seat of power and creation.

For at last, it is only that exceeding and universal part which interests us, when we shall read in a true history what befalls in that kingdom where a thousand years is as one day, and see that what is set down is true through all the sciences; in the laws of thought as well as of chemistry.

In all sciences the student is discovering that nature, as he calls it, is always working, in wholes and in every detail, after the laws of the human mind.[p. iii] Every creation, in parts or in particles, is on the method and by the means which our mind approves as soon as it is thoroughly acquainted with the facts; hence the delight. No matter how far or how high science explores, it adopts the method of the universe as fast as it appears; and this discloses that the mind as it opens, the mind as it shall be, comprehends and works thus; that is to say, the Intellect builds the universe and is the key to all it contains. *It is not then cities or mountains, or animals, or globes that any longer command us, but only man; not the fact but so much of man as is in the fact.*[p. iii]

In astronomy, vast distance, but we never go into a foreign system. In geology, vast duration, but we are never strangers. Our metaphysic should be able to follow the flying force through all transformations, and name the pair identical through all variety.

I believe in the existence of the material world as the expression of the spiritual or the real, and in the impenetrable mystery which hides (and hides through absolute transparency) the mental nature,[p. 4] I await the insight which our advancing knowledge of material laws shall furnish.

Every object in nature is a word to signify some fact in the mind. But when that fact is not yet put into English words, when I look at the tree or the river and have not yet definitely made out what they would say to me, they are by no means unimpressive. I wait for them, I enjoy them before they yet speak. I feel as if I stood by an ambassador charged with the message of his king, which he does not deliver because the hour when he should say it is not yet arrived.[p. 6]

Whilst we converse with truths as thoughts, they exist also as plastic forces; as the soul of a man, the soul of a plant, the genius or constitution of any part of nature, which makes it what it is. The thought which was in the world, part and parcel of the world, has disengaged itself and taken an independent existence.[p. 8]

My belief in the use of a course on philosophy is that the student shall learn to appreciate the miracle of the mind; shall learn its subtle but immense power, or shall begin to learn it; shall come to know that in seeing and in no tradition he must find what truth is; that he shall see in it the source of all traditions, and shall see each one of them as better or worse statement of its

revelations; shall come to trust it entirely, as the only true; to cleave to God against the name of God. When he has once known the oracle he will need no priest. And if he finds at first with some alarm how impossible it is to accept many things that the hot or the mild sectarian may insist on his believing, he will be armed by his insight and brave to meet all inconvenience and all resistance it may cost him. He from whose hand it came will guide and direct it.

Yet these questions that really interest men, how few can answer. Here are learned faculties of law and divinity, but would questions like these come into mind when I see them? Here are learned academies and universities, yet they have not propounded these for any prize.

Seek the literary circles, the stars of fame, the men of splendor, of bon–mots, will they afford me satisfaction? I think you could not find a club of men acute and liberal enough in the world. Bring the best wits together, and they are so impatient of each other, so vulgar, there is so much more than their wit, — such follies, gluttonies, partialities, age, care, and sleep, that you shall have no academy.

There is really a grievous amount of unavailableness about men of wit. A plain man finds them so heavy, dull and oppressive, with bad jokes and conceit and stupefying individualism, that he comes to write in his tablets, Avoid the great man as one who is privileged to be an unprofitable companion. For the course of things makes the scholars either egotists or worldly and jocose. In so many hundreds of superior men hardly ten or five or two from whom one can hope for a reasonable word.

Go into the scientific club and hearken. Each savant proves in his admirable discourse that he and he only knows now or ever did know anything on the subject: "Does the gentleman speak of anatomy? Who peeped into a box at the Custom House and then published a drawing of my rat?" Or is it pretended discoveries of new strata that are before the meeting? This professor hastens to inform us that he knew it all twenty years ago, and is ready to prove that he knew so much then that all further investigation was quite superfluous; — and poor nature and the sublime law, which is all that our student cares to hear of, are quite omitted in this triumphant vindication.

Was it better when we came to the philosophers, who found everybody wrong; acute and ingenious to lampoon and degrade mankind? And then was there ever prophet burdened with a message to his people who did not cloud our gratitude by a strange confounding in his own mind of private folly with his public wisdom?

But if you like to run away from this besetting sin of sedentary men, you can escape all this insane egotism by running into society, where the manners and estimate of the world have corrected this folly, and effectually suppressed this overweening self-conceit. Here each is to make room for others, and the solidest merits must exist only for the entertainment of all. We are not in the smallest degree helped. Great is the dazzle, but the gain is small. Here they play the game of conversation, as they play billiards, for pastime and credit. Yes, 't is a great vice in all countries, the sacrifice of scholars to be courtiers and diners-out, to talk for the amusement of those who wish to be amused, though the stars of heaven must be plucked down and packed into rockets to this end. What with egotism on one side and levity on the other we shall have no Olympus.

But there is still another hindrance, namely, practicality. We must have a special talent, and bring something to pass. Ever since the Norse heaven made the stern terms of admission that a man must do something excellent with his hands or feet, or with his voice, eyes, ears, or with his whole body, the same demand has been made in Norse earth.

Yet what we really want is not a haste to act, but a certain piety toward the source of action and knowledge. In fact we have to say that there is a certain beatitude, — I can call it nothing less,

— to which all men are entitled, tasted by them in different degrees, which is a perfection of their nature, and to which their entrance must be in every way forwarded. Practical men, though they could lift the globe, cannot arrive at this. Something very different has to be done, — the availing ourselves of every impulse of genius, an emanation of the heaven it tells of, and the resisting this conspiracy of men and material things against the sanitary and legitimate inspirations of the intellectual nature.

What is life but the angle of vision? A man is measured by the angle at which he looks at objects. What is life but what a man is thinking of all day? This is his fate and his employer. Knowing is the measure of the man. By how much we know, so much we are.

The laws and powers of the Intellect have, however, a stupendous peculiarity, of being at once observers and observed. So that it is difficult to hold them fast, as objects of examination, or hinder them from turning the professor out of his chair. The wonder of the science of Intellect is that the substance with which we deal is of that subtle and active quality that it intoxicates all who approach it. Gloves on the hands, glass guards over the eyes, wire–gauze masks over the face, volatile salts in the nostrils, are no defence against this virus, which comes in as secretly as gravitation into and through all barriers.

Let me have your attention to this dangerous subject, which we will cautiously approach on different sides of this dim and perilous lake, so attractive, so delusive. We have had so many guides and so many failures. And now the world is still uncertain whether the pool has been sounded or not.

My contribution will be simply historical. I write anecdotes of the intellect; a sort of Farmer's Almanac of mental moods. I confine my ambition to true reporting of its play in natural action, though I should get only one new fact in a year.

I cannot myself use that systematic form which is reckoned essential in treating the science of the mind. But if one can say so without arrogance, I might suggest that he who contents himself with dotting a fragmentary curve, recording only what facts he has observed, without attempting to arrange them within one outline, follows a system also, — a system as grand as any other, though he does not interfere with its vast curves by prematurely forcing them into a circle or ellipse, but only draws that arc which he clearly sees, or perhaps at a later observation a remote curve of the same orbit, and waits for a new opportunity, well assured that these observed arcs will consist with each other.

I confess to a little distrust of that completeness of system which metaphysicians are apt to affect. 'T is the gnat grasping the world. All these exhaustive theories appear indeed a false and vain attempt to introvert and analyze the Primal Thought. That is upstream, and what a stream! Can you swim up Niagara Falls?

We have invincible repugnance to introversion, to study of the eyes instead of that which the eyes see; and the belief of men is that the attempt is unnatural and is punished by loss of faculty. I share the belief that the natural direction of the intellectual powers is from within outward, and that just in proportion to the activity of thoughts on the study of outward objects, as architecture, or farming, or natural history, ships, animals, chemistry, — in that proportion the faculties of the mind had a healthy growth; but a study in the opposite direction had a damaging effect on the mind.

Metaphysic is dangerous as a single pursuit. We should feel more confidence in the same results from the mouth of a man of the world. The inward analysis must be corrected by rough experience. Metaphysics must be perpetually reinforced by life; must be the observations of a working man on working men; must be biography, — the record of some law whose working was surprised by the observer in natural action.

I think metaphysics a grammar to which, once read, we seldom return. 'T is a Manila full of pepper, and I want only a teaspoonful in a year. I admire the Dutch, who burned half the harvest to enhance the price of the remainder.

I want not the logic but the power, if any, which it brings into science and literature; the man who can humanize this logic, these syllogisms, and give me the results. The adepts value only the pure geometry, the aerial bridge ascending from earth to heaven with arches and abutments of pure reason. I am fully contented if you tell me where are the two termini.

My metaphysics are to the end of use. *I wish to know the laws of this wonderful power, that I may domesticate it. I observe with curiosity its risings and settings, illumination and eclipse; its obstructions and its provocations, that I may learn to live with it wisely, court its aid, catch sight of its splendor, feel its approach, hear and save its oracles and obey them.*[p. 10] But this watching of the mind, in season and out of season, to see the mechanics of the thing, is a little of the detective. The analytic process is cold and bereaving and, shall I say it? somewhat mean, as spying. There is something surgical in metaphysics as we treat it. Were not an ode a better form? The poet sees wholes and avoids analysis; the metaphysician, dealing as it were with the mathematics of the mind, puts himself out of the way of the inspiration; loses that which is the miracle and creates the worship.

I think that philosophy is still rude and elementary. It will one day be taught by poets. The poet is in the natural attitude; he is believing; the philosopher, after some struggle, having only reasons for believing.

What I am now to attempt is simply some sketches or studies for such a picture; Memoires pour servir toward a Natural History of Intellect.

First I wish to speak of the excellence of that element, and the great auguries that come from it, notwithstanding the impediments which our sensual civilization puts in the way.

Next I treat of the identity of the thought with Nature; and I add a rude list of some by–laws of the mind.

Thirdly I proceed to the fountains of thought in Instinct and Inspiration, and I also attempt to show the relation of men of thought to the existing religion and civility of the present time.

I

We figure to ourselves Intellect as an ethereal sea, which ebbs and flows, which surges and washes hither and thither, carrying its whole virtue into every creek and inlet which it bathes. To this sea every human house has a water front. But this force, creating nature, visiting whom it will and withdrawing from whom it will, making day where it comes and leaving night when it departs, is no fee or property of man or angel. It is as the light, public and entire to each, and on the same terms.

What but thought deepens life, and makes us better than cow or cat? The grandeur of the impression the stars and heavenly bodies make on us is surely more valuable than our exact perception of a tub or a table on the ground.

To Be is the unsolved, unsolvable wonder.[p. 18] *To Be, in its two connections of inward and outward, the mind and nature. The wonder subsists, and age, though of eternity, could not approach a solution.*[p. 20] But the suggestion is always returning, that hidden source publishing at once our being and that it is the source of outward nature. *Who are we and what is Nature have one answer in the life that rushes into us.*[p. 20]

In my thought I seem to stand on the bank of a river and watch the endless flow of the stream, floating objects of all shapes, colors and natures; nor can I much detain them as they pass, except by running beside them a little way along the bank. But whence they come or whither they go is not told me. Only I have a suspicion that, as geologists say every river makes its own valley, so does this mystic stream. It makes its valley, makes its banks and makes perhaps the observer too.[p. 12] *Who has found the boundaries of human intelligence? Who has made a chart of its channel or approached the fountain of this wonderful Nile?*[p. 14]

I am of the oldest religion. Leaving aside the question which was prior, egg or bird, *I believe the mind is the creator of the world, and is ever creating; — that at last Matter is dead Mind; that mind makes the senses it sees with; that the genius of man is a continuation of the power that made him and that has not done making him.*[p. 22]

I dare not deal with this element in its pure essence. It is too rare for the wings of words.[p. 30] Yet I see that Intellect is a science of degrees, and that as man is conscious of the law of vegetable and animal nature, so he is aware of an Intellect which overhangs his consciousness like a sky, of degree above degree, of heaven within heaven.

Every just thinker has attempted to indicate these degrees, these steps on the heavenly stair, until he comes to light where language fails him. *Above the thought is the higher truth,— truth as yet undomesticated and therefore unformulated.*[p. 28]

It is a steep stair down from the essence of Intellect pure to thoughts and intellections. As the sun is conceived to have made our system by hurling out from itself the outer rings of diffuse ether which slowly condensed into earths and moons, by a higher force of the same law

the mind detaches minds, and a mind detaches thoughts or intellections. These again all mimic in their sphericity the first mind, and share its power.

Life is incessant parturition.[p. 24] There are viviparous and oviparous minds; minds that produce their thoughts complete men, like armed soldiers, ready and swift to go out to resist and conquer all the armies of error, and others that deposit their dangerous unripe thoughts here and there to lie still for a time and be brooded in other minds, and the shell not be broken until the next age, for them to begin, as new individuals, their career.

The perceptions of a soul, its wondrous progeny, are born by the conversation, the marriage of souls; so nourished, so enlarged. They are detached from their parent, they pass into other minds; ripened and unfolded by many they hasten to incarnate themselves in action, to take body, only to carry forward the will which sent them out. They take to themselves wood and stone and iron; ships and cities and nations and armies of men and ages of duration; the pomps of religion, the armaments of war, the codes and heraldry of states; agriculture, trade, commerce; — these are the ponderous instrumentalities into which the nimble thoughts pass, and which they animate and alter, and presently, antagonized by other thoughts which they first aroused, or by thoughts which are sons and daughters of these, the thought buries itself in the new thought of larger scope, whilst the old instrumentalities and incarnations are decomposed and recomposed into new.

Our eating, trading, marrying, and learning are mistaken by us for ends and realities, whilst they are properly symbols only; when we have come, by a divine leading, into the inner firmament, we are apprised of the unreality or representative character of what we esteemed final.

So works the poor little blockhead manikin. He must arrange and dignify his shop or farm the best he can. At last he must be able to tell you it, or write it, translate it all clumsily enough into the new sky–language he calls thought. He cannot help it, the irresistible meliorations bear him forward.

II

Whilst we consider this appetite of the mind to arrange its phenomena, there is another fact which makes this useful. *There is in nature a parallel unity which corresponds to the unity in the mind and makes it available.*[p. 32] This methodizing mind meets no resistance in its attempts. The scattered blocks, with which it strives to form a symmetrical structure, fit. This design following after finds with joy that like design went before. *Not only man puts things in a row, but things belong in a row.*[p. 32]

It is certain that however we may conceive of the wonderful little bricks of which the world is builded, we must suppose a similarity and fitting and identity in their frame. It is necessary to suppose that every hose in nature fits every hydrant; so only is combination, chemistry, vegetation, animation, intellection possible. *Without identity at base, chaos must be forever.*[p. 34]

And as mind, our mind or mind like ours reappears to us in our study of nature, nature being everywhere formed after a method which we can well understand, and all the parts, to the most remote, allied or explicable, — *therefore our own organization is a perpetual key, and a well–ordered mind brings to the study of every new fact or class of facts a certain divination of that which it shall find.*[p. 38]

This reduction to a few laws, to one law, is not a choice of the individual, it is the tyrannical instinct of the mind. There is no solitary flower and no solitary thought.[p. 40] It comes single like a foreign traveller, — but find out its name and it is related to a powerful and numerous family. Wonderful is their working and relation each to each. We hold them as lanterns to light each other and our present design. Every new thought modifies, interprets old problems. The retrospective value of each new thought is immense, like a torch applied to a long train of gunpowder. *To be isolated is to be sick, and in so far, dead. The life of the All must stream through us to make the man and the moment great.*[p. 42]

Well, having accepted this law of identity pervading the universe, we next perceive that whilst every creature represents and obeys it, there is diversity, there is more or less of power; that the lowest only means incipient form, and over it is a higher class in which its rudiments are opened, raised to higher powers; that there is development from less to more, from lower to superior function, steadily ascending to man.

If man has organs for breathing, for sight, for locomotion, for taking food, for digesting, for protection by house–building, by attack and defence, for reproduction and love and care of his young, you shall find all the same in the muskrat. There is a perfect correspondence;[p. 44] or 't is only man modified to live in a mud–bank. A fish in like manner is man furnished to live in the sea; a thrush, to fly in the air; and a mollusk is a cheap edition with a suppression of the costlier illustrations, designed for dingy circulation, for shelving in an oyster–bank or among the seaweed.

If we go through the British Museum or the Jardin des Plantes in Paris, or any cabinet where is some representation of all the kingdoms of nature, we are surprised with occult sympathies; we feel as if looking at our own bone and flesh through coloring and distorting glasses.[p. 46] Is it not a little startling to see with what genius some people take to hunting, with what genius some people fish, — what knowledge they still have of the creature they hunt? The robber, as the police reports say, must have been intimately acquainted with the premises. How lately the hunter was the poor creature's organic enemy; a presumption inflamed, as the lawyers say, by observing how many faces in the street still remind us of visages in the forest, — the escape from the quadruped type not yet perfectly accomplished.

From whatever side we look at Nature we seem to be exploring the figure of a disguised man.[p. 48] How obvious is the momentum in our mental history! The momentum, which increases by exact laws in falling bodies, increases by the same rate in the intellectual action. Every scholar knows that he applies himself coldly and slowly at first to his task, but, with the progress of the work, the mind itself becomes heated, and sees far and wide as it approaches the end, so that it is the common remark of the student, Could I only have begun with the same fire which I had on the last day, I should have done something.

The affinity of particles accurately translates the affinity of thoughts, and what a modern experimenter calls "the contagious influence of chemical action" is so true of mind that I have only to read the law that its application may be evident: "A body in the act of combination or decomposition enables another body, with which it may be in contact, to enter into the same state." And if one remembers how contagious are the moral states of men, how much we are braced by the presence and actions of any Spartan soul; it does not need vigor of our own kind, but the spectacle of vigor of any kind, any prodigious power of performance wonderfully arms and recruits us. There are those who disputing will make you dispute, and the nervous and hysterical and animalized will produce a like series of symptoms in you, though no other persons ever evoke the like phenomena, and though you are conscious that they do not properly belong to you, but are a sort of extension of the diseases of this particular person into you.

The idea of vegetation is irresistible in considering mental activity. Man seems a higher plant. What happens here in mankind is matched by what happens out there in the history of grass and wheat. This curious resemblance repeats, in the mental function, the germination, growth, state of melioration, crossings, blight, parasites, and in short all the accidents of the plant. Under every leaf is the bud of a new leaf, and not less under every thought is a newer thought. The plant absorbs much nourishment from the ground in order to repair its own waste by exhalation, and keep itself good. Increase its food and it becomes fertile. The mind is first only receptive. Surcharge it with thoughts in which it delights and it becomes active. The moment a man begins not to be convinced, that moment he begins to convince.

In the orchard many trees send out a moderate shoot in the first summer heat, and stop. They look all summer as if they would presently burst into bud again, but they do not. The fine tree continues to grow. The same thing happens in the man. Every man has material enough in his experience to exhaust the sagacity of Newton in working it out. We have more than we use. I never hear a good speech at caucus or at cattle–show but it helps me, not so much by adding to my knowledge as by apprising me of admirable uses to which what I know can be turned. The commonest remark, if the man could only extend it a little, would make him a genius; but the thought is prematurely checked, and grows no more. All great masters are chiefly distinguished by the power of adding a second, a third, and perhaps a fourth step in a continuous line. Many a man had taken their first step. With every additional step you enhance immensely the value of your first.

The botanist discovered long ago that Nature loves mixtures, and that nothing grows well on the crab–stock, but the blood of two trees being mixed a new and excellent fruit is produced. And not less in human history aboriginal races are incapable of improvement; the dull, melancholy Pelasgi[26] arrive at no civility until the Phoenicians and Ionians come in. The Briton, the Pict, is nothing until the Roman, the Saxon, the Norman, arrives.

It is observed that our mental processes go forward even when they seem suspended. Scholars say that if they return to the study of a new language after some intermission, the intelligence of it is more and not less. A subject of thought to which we return from month to month, from year to year, has always some ripeness of which we can give no account. We say the book grew in the author's mind.

In unfit company the finest powers are paralyzed. No ambition, no opposition, no friendly attention and fostering kindness, no wine, music or exhilarating aids, neither warm fireside nor fresh air, walking or riding, avail at all to resist the palsy of mis–association. Genius is mute, is dull; there is no genius. Ask of your flowers to open when you have let in on them a freezing wind.

The mechanical laws might as easily be shown pervading the kingdom of mind as the vegetative. A man has been in Spain. The facts and thoughts which the traveller has found in that country gradually settle themselves into a determinate heap of one size and form and not another. That is what he knows and has to say of Spain; he cannot say it truly until a sufficient time for the arrangement of the particles has elapsed.

These views of the source of thought and the mode of its communication lead us to a whole system of ethics, strict as any department of human duty, and open to us the tendencies and duties of men of thought in the present time.

Wisdom is like electricity. There is no permanent wise man, but men capable of wisdom, who being put into certain company or other favorable conditions become wise, as glasses rubbed acquire power for a time.

An individual body is the momentary arrest or fixation of certain atoms, which, after performing compulsory duty to this enchanted statue, are released again to flow in the currents of the world. An individual mind in like manner is a fixation or momentary eddy in which certain services and powers are taken up and minister in petty niches and localities, and then, being released, return to the unbounded soul of the world.

In this eternal resurrection and rehabilitation of transitory persons, who and what are they? 'T is only the source that we can see; — the eternal mind, careless of its channels, omnipotent in itself, and continually ejaculating its torrent into every artery and vein and veinlet of humanity. Wherever there is health, that is, consent to the cause and constitution of the universe, there is perception and power.

Each man is a new power in Nature. He holds the keys of the world in his hands. No quality in Nature's vast magazines he cannot touch, no truth he cannot see. Silent, passive, even sulkily Nature offers every morning her wealth to man. She is immensely rich; he is welcome to her entire goods, but she speaks no word, will not so much as beckon or cough; only this, she is careful to leave all her doors ajar,[p. 52] — towers, hall, storeroom and cellar. If he takes her hint and uses her goods she speaks no word; if he blunders and starves she says nothing. To the idle blockhead Nature is poor, sterile, inhospitable. To the gardener her loam is all strawberries, pears, pineapples. To the miller her rivers whirl the wheel and weave carpets and broadcloth. To the sculptor her stone is soft; to the painter her plumbago and marl are pencils and chromes. To the poet all sounds and words are melodies and rhythms. *In her hundred-gated Thebes every chamber is a new door.*[p. 52]

But he enters the world by one key. Herein is the wealth of each. His equipment, though new, is complete; his prudence is his own; his courage, his charity, are his own. He has his own defenses and his own fangs; his perception and his own mode of reply to sophistries. Whilst he draws on his own he cannot be overshadowed or supplanted.

There are two mischievous superstitions, I know not which does the most harm, one, that "I am wiser than you," and the other that "You are wiser than I." The truth is that every man is furnished, if he will heed it, with wisdom necessary to steer his own boat, — if he will not look away from his own to see how his neighbor steers his.[p. 54]

Every man is a new method and distributes things anew. If he could attain full size he would take up, first or last, atom by atom, all the world into a new form.[p. 58] And our deep conviction of the riches proper to every mind does not allow us to admit of much looking over into one another's virtues. Let me whisper a secret; nobody ever forgives any admiration in you of them, any overestimate of what they do or have. I acquiesce to be that I am, but I wish no one to be civil to me.

Strong men understand this very well. Power fraternizes with power, and wishes you not to be like him but like yourself. *Echo the leaders and they will fast enough see that you have nothing for them. They came to you for something they had not.* [p. 56]

There is always a loss of truth and power when a man leaves working for himself to work for another. Absolutely speaking I can only work for myself. All my good is magnetic, and I educate not by lessons but by going about my business. When, moved by love, a man teaches his child or joins with his neighbor in any act of common benefit, or spends himself for his friend, or rushes at immense personal sacrifice on some public, self–immolating act, it is not done for others, but to fulfil a high necessity of his proper character. The benefit to others is contingent and not contemplated by the doer.

The one thing not to be forgiven to intellectual persons is that they believe in the ideas of others. From this deference comes the imbecility and fatigue of their society, for of course they cannot affirm these from the deep life; they say what they would have you believe, but what they do not quite know. Profound sincerity is the only basis of talent as of character. The temptation is to patronize Providence, to fall into the accepted ways of talking and acting of the good sort of people.

Each has a certain aptitude for knowing or doing somewhat which, when it appears, is so adapted and aimed on that, that it seems a sort of obtuseness to everything else. Well, this aptitude, if he would obey it, would prove a telescope to bring under his clear vision what was blur to everybody else. 'T is a wonderful instrument, an organic sympathy with the whole frame of things. There is no property or relation in that immense arsenal of forces which the earth is, but some man is at last found who affects this, delights to unfold and work it, as if he were the born publisher and demonstrator of it.

As a dog has a sense that you have not, to find the track of his master or of a fox, and as each tree can secrete from the soil the elements that form a peach, a lemon, or a cocoa–nut, according to its kind, so individual men have secret senses, each some incommunicable sagacity. And men are primary or secondary as their opinions and actions are organic or not.

I know well what a sieve every ear is. Teach me never so much and I bear or retain only that which I wish to hear, what comports with my experience and my desire. Many eyes go through the meadow, but few see the flowers. A hunter finds plenty of game on the ground you have sauntered over with idle gun. White huckleberries are so rare that in miles of pasture you shall not find a dozen. But a girl who understands it will find you a pint in a quarter of an hour.

Though the world is full of food we can take only the crumbs fit for us. The air rings with sounds, but only a few vibrations can reach our tympanum. Perhaps creatures live with us which we never see, because their motion is too swift for our vision. The sun may shine, or a galaxy of suns; you will get no more light than your eye will hold. What can Plato or Newton teach, if you are deaf or incapable? A mind does not receive truth as a chest receives jewels that are put into it, but as the stomach takes up food into the system. It is no longer food, but flesh, and is assimilated. The appetite and the power of digestion measure our right to knowledge. He has it who can use it. As soon as our accumulation overruns our invention or power to use, the evils of intellectual gluttony begin, — congestion of the brain, apoplexy and strangulation.

III

In reckoning the sources of our mental power it were fatal to omit that one which pours all the others into its mould; — that unknown country in which all the rivers of our knowledge have their fountains, and which, by its qualities and structure, determines both the nature of the waters and the direction in which they flow.[p. 62]

The healthy mind lies parallel to the currents of nature and sees things in place, or makes discoveries.[p. 64] Newton did not exercise more ingenuity but less than another to see the world. *Right thought comes spontaneously, comes like the morning wind; comes daily, like our daily bread, to humble service; comes duly to those who look for it. It does not need to pump your brains and force thought to think rightly.* [p. 159] Oh no, the ingenious person is warped by his ingenuity and mis–sees.

Instinct is our name for the potential wit. Each man has a feeling that what is done any-where is done by the same wit as his. All men are his representatives, and he is glad to see that his wit can work at this or that problem as it ought to be done, and better than he could do it. We feel as if one man wrote all the books, painted, built, in dark ages; and we are sure that it can do more than ever was done. It was the same mind that built the world. That is Instinct.

Ask what the Instinct declares, and we have little to say. He is no newsmonger, no disputant, no talker. 'T is a taper, a spark in the great night. Yet a spark at which all the illuminations of human arts and sciences were kindled. This is that glimpse of inextin-guishable light by which men are guided; though it does not show objects, yet it shows the way.[p. 66] This is that sense by which men feel when they are wronged, though they do not see how. This is that source of thought and feeling which acts on masses of men, on all men at certain times, with resistless power. Ever at intervals leaps a word or fact to light which is no man's invention, but the common instinct, making the revolutions that never go back.

This is Instinct, and Inspiration is only this power excited, breaking its silence; the spark bursting into flame.[p. 70] *Instinct is a shapeless giant in the cave, massive, without hands or fingers or articulating lips or teeth or tongue; Behemoth, disdaining speech, disdaining particulars, lurking, surly, invincible, disdaining thoughts, always whole, never distributed, aboriginal, old as nature, and saying, like poor Topsy,*[27] *"never was born; growed." Indifferent to the dignity of its function, it plays the god in animal nature as in human or as in the angelic, and spends its omniscience on the lowest wants.*[p. 68] The old Hindoo Gautama says, "Like the approach of the iron to the loadstone is the approach of the new–born child to the breast." There is somewhat awful in that first approach.

The Instinct begins at this low point, at the surface of the earth, and works for the necessities of the human being; then ascends step by step to suggestions which are when expressed the intellectual and moral laws.

The mythology cleaves close to nature; and what else was it they represented in Pan, god of shepherds, who was not yet completely finished in godlike form, blocked rather, and wanting the extremities; had emblematic horns and feet? Pan, that is, All. His habit was to dwell in mountains, lying on the ground, tooting like a cricket in the sun, refusing to speak, clinging to his behemoth ways. He could intoxicate by the strain of his shepherd's pipe, — silent yet to most, for his pipes make the music of the spheres, which because it sounds eternally is not heard at all by the dull, but only by the mind. He wears a coat of leopard spots or stars. He could terrify by earth–born fears called panics. Yet was he in the secret of nature and could look both before and after. He was only seen under disguises, and was not represented by any outward image; a terror sometimes, at others a placid omnipotence.

Such homage did the Greek, — delighting in accurate form, not fond of the extravagant and unbounded — pay to the inscrutable force we call Instinct, or nature when it first becomes intelligent.

The action of the Instinct is for the most part negative, regulative, rather than initiative or impulsive. But it has a range as wide as human nature, running over all the ground of morals, of intellect, and of sense. In its lower function, when it deals with the apparent world, it is common sense. It requires the performance of all that is needful to the animal life and health. Then it requires a proportion between a man's acts and his condition, requires all that is called humanity; that symmetry and connection which is imperative in all healthily constituted men, and the want of which the rare and brilliant sallies of irregular genius cannot excuse.

If we could retain our early innocence we might trust our feet uncommanded to take the right path to our friend in the woods. But we have interfered too often; the feet have lost, by our distrust, their proper virtue, and we take the wrong path and miss him. 'T is the barbarian instinct within us which culture deadens.

We find ourselves expressed in nature, but we cannot translate it into words. But Perception is the armed eye. A civilization has tamed and ripened this savage wit, and he is a Greek. His Aye and No have become nouns and verbs and adverbs. Perception differs from Instinct by adding the Will. Simple percipiency is the virtue of space, not of man.

The senses minister to a mind they do not know. *At a moment in our history the mind's eye opens and we become aware of spiritual facts, of rights, of duties, of thoughts, — a thousand faces of one essence. We call the essence Truth; the particular aspects of it we call thoughts. These facts, this essence, are not new; they are old and eternal, but our seeing of them is new. Having seen them we are no longer brute lumps whirled by Fate, but we pass into the council–chamber and government of nature. In so far as we see them we share their life and sovereignty.*[p. 72]

The point of interest is here, that these gates, once opened, never swing back. The observers may come at their leisure, and do at last satisfy themselves of the fact. The thought, the doctrine, the right hitherto not affirmed is published in set propositions, in conversation of scholars and philosophers, of men of the world, and at last in the very choruses of songs. The young hear it, and as they have never fought it, never known it otherwise, they accept it, vote for it at the polls, embody it in the laws. And the perception thus satisfied reacts on the senses, to clarify them, so that it becomes more indisputable.

This is the first property of the Intellect I am to point out; the mind detaches. A man is intellectual in proportion as he can make an object of every sensation, perception and intuition;[p. 76] so long as he has no engagement in any thought or feeling which can hinder him from looking at it as somewhat foreign.

A man of talent has only to name any form or fact with which we are most familiar, and the strong light which he throws on it enhances it to all eyes.

People wonder they never saw it before. The detachment consists in seeing it under a new order, not under a personal but under a universal light. To us it had economic, but to the universe it has poetic relations, and it is as good as sun and star now.[p. 78] Indeed this is the measure of all intellectual power among men, the power to complete this detachment, the power of genius to hurl a new individual into the world.

An intellectual man has the power to go out of himself and see himself as an object; therefore his defects and delusions interest him as much as his successes. He not only wishes to succeed in life, but he wishes in thought to know the history and destiny of a man; whilst the cloud of egotists drifting about are only interested in a success to their egotism.

The senses report the new fact or change; the mind discovers some essential copula binding this fact or change to a class of facts or changes, and enjoys the discovery as if coming to its own again. *A perception is always a generalization. It lifts the object, whether in material or moral nature, into a type. The animal, the low degrees of intellect, know only individuals. The philosopher knows only laws.*[p. 80] That is, he considers a purely mental fact, part of the soul itself. We say with Kenelm Digby,[28] "All things that she knoweth are herself, and she is all that she knoweth." *Insight assimilates the thing seen. Is it only another way of affirming and illustrating this to say that it sees nothing alone, but sees each particular object in just connections, — sees all in God?*[p. 82] In all healthy souls is an inborn necessity of presupposing for each particular fact a prior Being which compels it to a harmony with all other natures. The game of Intellect is the perception that whatever befalls or can be stated is a universal proposition; and contrariwise, that every general statement is poetical again by being particularized or impersonated.

A single thought has no limit to its value; a thought, properly speaking, — that is a truth held not from any man's saying so, or any accidental benefit or recommendation it has in our trade or circumstance, but because we have perceived it is a fact in the nature of things, and in all times and places will and must be the same thing, — is of inestimable value.[p. 84] Every new impression on the mind is not to be derided, but is to be accounted for, and, until accounted for, registered as an indisputable addition to our catalogue of natural facts.

The first fact is the fate in every mental perception, — that my seeing this or that, and that I see it so or so, is as much a fact in the natural history of the world as is the freezing of water at thirty-two degrees of Fahrenheit. My percipiency affirms the presence and perfection of law, as much as all the martyrs. *A perception, it is of a necessity older than the sun and moon, and the Father of the Gods.*[p. 86] It is there with all its destinies. It is its nature to rush to expression, to rush to embody itself. It is impatient to put on its sandals and be gone on its errand, which is to lead to a larger perception, and so to new action. For thought exists to be expressed. That which cannot externize itself is not thought.

Do not trifle with your perceptions, or hold them cheap. They are your door to the seven heavens,[p. 88] and if you pass it by you will miss your way: Say, what impresses me ought to impress me. I am bewildered by the immense variety of attractions and cannot take a step; but this one thread, fine as gossamer, is yet real; and I hear a whisper, which I dare trust, that it is the thread on which the earth and the heaven of heavens are strung.

The universe is traversed by paths or bridges or stepping–stones across the gulfs of space in every direction. To every soul that is created is its path, invisible to all but itself.[p. 92] Each soul, therefore, walking in its own path walks firmly; and to the astonishment of all other souls, who see not its path, it goes as softly and playfully on its way as if, instead of being a line, narrow as the edge of a sword, over terrific pits right and left, it were a wide prairie.

Genius is a delicate sensibility to the laws of the world, adding the power to express them again in some new form.[p. 94] The highest measure of poetic power is such insight and faculty to fuse the circumstances of to–day as shall make transparent the whole web of circumstance and opinion in which the man finds himself, so that he releases himself from the traditions in which he grew, — no longer looks back to Hebrew or Greek or English use or tradition in religion, laws, or life, but sees so truly the omnipresence of eternal cause that he can convert the daily and hourly event of New York, of Boston, into universal symbols. *I owe to genius always the same debt, of lifting the curtain from the common and showing me that gods are sitting disguised in every company.*[p. 96]

The conduct of Intellect must respect nothing so much as preserving the sensibility. *My measure for all subjects of science as of events is their impression on the soul.*[p. 98] That mind is best which is most impressionable. *There are times when the cawing of a crow, a weed, a snow–flake, a boy's willow whistle, or a farmer planting in his field is more suggestive to the mind than the Yosemite gorge or the Vatican would be in another hour.*[p. 98] In like mood an old verse, or certain words, gleam with rare significance.

But sensibility does not exhaust our idea of it. That is only half. Genius is not a lazy angel contemplating itself and things. It is insatiable for expression. Thought must take the stupendous step of passing into realization. A master can formulate his thought. Our thoughts at first possess us. Later, if we have good heads, we come to possess them.[p. 100] We believe that certain persons add to the common vision a certain degree of control over these states of mind; that the true scholar is one who has the power to stand beside his thoughts or to hold off his thoughts at arm's length and give them perspective.

It is not to be concealed that the gods have guarded this privilege with costly penalty. This slight discontinuity which perception effects between the mind and the object paralyzes the will. If you cut or break in two a block or stone and press the two parts closely together, you can indeed bring the particles very near, but never again so near that they shall attract each other so that you can take up the block as one. That indescribably small interval is as good as a thousand miles, and has forever severed the practical unity. Such is the immense deduction from power by discontinuity.

The intellect that sees the interval partakes of it, and the fact of intellectual perception severs once for all the man from the things with which he converses. Affection blends, intellect disjoins subject and object. For weal or woe we clear ourselves from the thing we contemplate. We grieve but are not the grief; we love but are not love. If we converse with low things, with crimes, with mischances, we are not compromised. And if with high things, with heroic actions, with virtues, the interval becomes a gulf and we cannot enter into the highest good. Artist natures do not weep. Goethe, the surpassing intellect of modern times, apprehends the spiritual but is not spiritual.

There is indeed this vice about men of thought, that you cannot quite trust them; not as much as other men of the same natural probity, without intellect; because they have a hankering to play Providence and make a distinction in favor of themselves from the rules they apply to the human race.

The primary rule for the conduct of Intellect is to have control of the thoughts without losing their natural attitudes and action. They are the oracle; we are not to poke and drill and force, but to follow them. Yet the spirits of the prophets are subject to the prophets. You must formulate your thought or 't is all sky and no stars. There are men of great apprehension, discursive minds, who easily entertain ideas, but are not exact, severe with themselves, cannot connect or arrange their thoughts so as effectively to report them. A blending of these two — the intellectual perception of truth and the moral sentiment of right — is wisdom. All thought is practical. Wishing is one thing; will another. Wishing is castle–building; the dreaming about things agreeable to the senses, but to which we have no right. Will is the advance to that which rightly belongs to us, to which the inward magnet ever points, and which we dare to make ours. The revelation of thought takes us out of servitude into freedom. So does the sense of right.

Will is the measure of power. To a great genius there must be a great will. If the thought is not a lamp to the will, does not proceed to an act, the wise are imbecile. He alone is strong and happy who has a will. The rest are herds. He uses; they are used. He is of the Maker; they are of the Made.

Will is always miraculous, being the presence of God to men. [p. 104] When it appears in a man he is a hero, and all metaphysics are at fault. Heaven is the exercise of the faculties, the added sense of power.

All men know the truth, but what of that? It is rare to find one who knows how to speak it. A man tries to speak it and his voice is like the hiss of a snake, or rude and chiding. The truth is not spoken but injured. The same thing happens in power to do the right. His rectitude is ridiculous. His organs do not play him true.

There is a meter which determines the constructive power of man, — this, namely, the question whether the mind possesses the control of its thoughts, or they of it. The new sect stands for certain thoughts. We go to individual members for an exposition of them. Vain expectation. They are possessed by the ideas but do not possess them. [p. 106] One meets contemplative men who dwell in a certain feeling and delight which are intellectual but wholly above their expression. They cannot formulate. They impress those who know them by their loyalty to the truth they worship but cannot impart. Sometimes the patience and love are rewarded by the chamber of power being at last opened; but sometimes they pass away dumb, to find it where all obstruction is removed.

By and by comes a facility; some one that can move the mountain and build of it a causeway through the Dismal Swamp, as easily as he carries the hair on his head. Talent is habitual facility of execution. We like people who can do things. The various talents are organic, or each related to that part of nature it is to explore and utilize. Somewhat is to come to the light, and one was created to fetch it, — a vessel of honor or of dishonor. 'T is of instant use in the economy of the Cosmos, and the more armed and biassed for the work the better.

Each of these talents is born to be unfolded and set at work for the use and delight of men, and, in the last result, the man with the talent is the need of mankind; the whole ponderous machinery of the state has really for its aim just to place this skill of each.

But idea and execution are not often entrusted to the same head. There is some incompatibility of good speculation and practice, for example, the failure of monasteries and Brook Farms.[29] To hammer out phalanxes must be done by smiths; as soon as the scholar attempts it he is half a charlatan.

The grasp is the main thing. Most men's minds do not grasp anything. All slips through their fingers, like the paltry brass grooves that in most country houses are used to raise or drop the curtain, but are made to sell, and will not hold any curtain but cobwebs. I have heard that idiot children are known from their birth by the circumstance that their hands do not close round anything. Webster naturally and always grasps, and therefore retains something from every company and circumstance.

As a talent Dante's imagination is the nearest to hands and feet that we have seen. He clasps the thought as if it were a tree or a stone, and describes as mathematically. I once found Page[30] the painter modeling his figures in clay, Ruth and Naomi, before he painted them on canvas. Dante, one would say, did the same thing before he wrote the verses.

I have spoken of Intellect constructive. But it is in degrees. How it moves when its pace is accelerated! The pace of Nature is so slow. Why not from strength to strength, from miracle to miracle, and not as now with this retardation — as if Nature had sprained her foot — and plenteous stopping at little stations?

The difference is obvious enough in Talent between the speed of one man's action above another's. In debate, in legislature, not less in action; in war or in affairs, alike daring and effective. But I speak of it in quite another sense, namely, in the habitual speed of combination of thought.

The same functions which are perfect in our quadrupeds are seen slower performed in palaeontology. Many races it cost them to achieve the completion that is now in the life of one. Life had not yet so fierce a glow.

Shakespeare astonishes by his equality in every play, act, scene or line. One would say he must have been a thousand years old when he wrote his first line, so thoroughly is his thought familiar to him, and has such scope and so solidly worded, as if it were already a proverb and not hereafter to become one. [p. 108] Well, that millenium in effect is really only a little acceleration in his process of thought.

But each power is commonly at the expense of some other. When pace is increased it will happen that the control is in a degree lost. Reason does not keep her firm seat. The Delphian prophetess,[31] when the spirit possesses her, is herself a victim. The excess of individualism, when it is not corrected or subordinated to the Supreme Reason, makes that vice which we stigmatize as monotones, men of one idea, or, as the French say, enfant perdu d'une conviction isolée,[32] which give such a comic tinge to all society. Every man has his theory, true, but ridiculously overstated. We are forced to treat a great part of mankind as if they were a little deranged. We detect their mania and humor it, so that conversation soon becomes a tiresome effort.

You laugh at the monotones, at the men of one idea, but if we look nearly at heroes we may find the same poverty; and perhaps it is not poverty, but power. *The secret of power, intellectual or physical, is concentration, and all concentration involves of necessity a certain narrowness.* [p. 110] It is a law of nature that he who looks at one thing must turn his eyes from every other thing in the universe. The horse goes better with blinders, and the man for dedication to his task. *If you ask what compensation is made for the inevitable narrowness, why, this, that in learning one thing well you learn all things.* [p. 110]

Immense is the patience of Nature. You say thought is a penurious rill.[33] Well, we can wait.

Nature is immortal, and can wait. Nature having for capital this rill, drop by drop, as it trickles from the rock of ages, — this rill and her patience, — she husbands and hives, she forms reservoirs, were it only a phial or a hair–tube that will hold as it were a drop of attar.[34] Not having enough to support all the powers of a race, she thins her stock and raises a few individuals, or only a pair. Not sufficing to feed all the faculties synchronously, she feeds one faculty and starves all the rest. I am familiar with cases, we meet them daily, wherein the vital force being insufficient for the constitution, everything is neglected that can be spared; some one power fed, all the rest pine. 'T is like a withered hand or leg on a Hercules. It makes inconvenience in society, for we presume symmetry, and because they know one thing we defer to them in another, and find them really contemptible. We can't make half a bow and say, I honor and despise you. But Nature can; she whistles with all her winds, and does as she pleases.

It is much to write sentences; it is more to add method and write out the spirit of your life symmetrically. But to arrange general reflections in their natural order, so that I shall have one homogeneous piece, — a Lycidas,[35] an Allegro, a Hamlet, a Midsummer Night's Dream, — this continuity is for the great. The wonderful men are wonderful hereby. Such concentration of experiences is in every great work, which, though successive in the mind of the master, were primarily combined in his piece.

But what we want is consecutiveness. 'T is with us a flash of light, then a long darkness, then a flash again. Ah! could we turn these fugitive sparkles into an astronomy of Copernican worlds.

I must think this keen sympathy, this thrill of awe with which we watch the performance of genius, a sign of our own readiness to exert the like power. *I must think we are entitled to powers far transcending any that we possess; that we have in the race the sketch of a man which no individual comes up to.* [p. 112]

Every sincere man is right, or, to make him right, only needs a little larger dose of his own personality. [p. 114] Excellent in his own way by means of not apprehending the gift of another. When he speaks out of another's mind, we detect it. He can't make any paint stick but his own. No man passes for that with another which he passes for with himself. The respect and the censure of his brother are alike injurious and irrelevant. We see ourselves; we lack organs to see others, and only squint at them.

Don't fear to push these individualities to their farthest divergence. Characters and talents are complemental and suppletory. The world stands by balanced antagonisms. The more the peculiarities are pressed the better the result. The air would rot without lightning; and without the violence of direction that men have, without bigots, without men of fixed idea, no excitement, no efficiency.

The novelist should not make any character act absurdly, but only absurdly as seen by others. For it is so in life. Nonsense will not keep its unreason if you come into the humorist's point of view, but unhappily we find it is fast becoming sense, and we must flee again into the distance if we would laugh.

What strength belongs to every plant and animal in nature. *The tree or the brook has no duplicity, no pretentiousness, no show. It is, with all its might and main, what it is, and makes one and the same impression and effect at all times.* [p. 116] All the thoughts of a turtle are turtles, and of a rabbit, rabbits. But a man is broken and dissipated by the giddiness of his will; he does not throw himself into his judgments; his genius leads him one way but 't is likely his trade or politics in quite another. He rows with one hand and with the other backs water, and does not give to any manner of life the strength of his constitution. Hence the perpetual loss of power and waste of human life.

The natural remedy against this miscellany of knowledge and aim, this desultory universality of ours, this immense ground–juniper falling abroad and not gathered up into any columnar tree, is to substitute realism for sentimentalism; a certain recognition of the simple and terrible laws which, seen or unseen, pervade and govern.

You will say this is quite axiomatic and a little too true. I do not find it an agreed point. Literary men for the most part have a settled despair as to the realization of ideas in their own time. There is in all students a distrust of truth, a timidity about affirming it; a wish to patronize Providence.

We disown our debt to moral evil. To science there is no poison; to botany no weed; to chemistry no dirt. The curses of malignity and despair are important criticism, which must be heeded until he can explain and rightly silence them.

"Croyez moi, l'erreur ausi a son mérite,"[36] said Voltaire. We see those who surmount by dint of egotism or infatuation obstacles from which the prudent recoil. The right partisan is a heady man, who, because he does not see many things, sees some one thing with heat and exaggeration; and if he falls among other narrow men, or objects which have a brief importance, prefers it to the universe, and seems inspired and a godsend to those who wish to magnify the matter and carry

a point. 'T is the difference between progress by railroad and by walking across the broken country. Immense speed, but only in one direction.

There are two theories of life; one for the demonstration of our talent, the other for the education of the man. One is activity, the busy–body, the following of that practical talent which we have, in the belief that what is so natural, easy and pleasant to us and desirable to others will surely lead us out safely; in this direction lie usefulness, comfort, society, low power of all sorts. The other is trust, religion, consent to be nothing for eternity, entranced waiting, the worship of ideas. This is solitary, grand, secular. They are in perpetual balance and strife. One is talent, the other genius. One is skill, the other character.

We are continually tempted to sacrifice genius to talent, the hope and promise of insight to the lust of a freer demonstration of those gifts we have; and we buy this freedom to glitter by the loss of general health.

It is the levity of this country to forgive everything to talent. If a man show cleverness, rhetorical skill, bold front in the forum or the senate, people clap their hands without asking more. We have a juvenile love of smartness, of showy speech. We like faculty that can rapidly be coined into money, and society seems to be in conspiracy to utilize every gift prematurely, and pull down genius to lucrative talent. Every kind of meanness and mischief is forgiven to intellect. All is condoned if I can write a good song or novel.

Wide is the gulf between genius and talent. The men we know, poets, wits, writers, deal with their thoughts as jewellers with jewels, which they sell but must not wear. Like the carpenter, who gives up the key of the fine house he has built, and never enters it again.

There is a conflict between a man's private dexterity or talent and his access to the free air and light which wisdom is; between wisdom and the habit and necessity of repeating itself which belongs to every mind. Peter is the mould into which everything is poured like warm wax, and be it astronomy or railroads or French revolution or theology or botany, it comes out Peter. But there are quick limits to our interest in the personality of people. They are as much alike as their barns and pantries, and are as soon musty and dreary. They entertain us for a time, but at the second or third encounter we have nothing more to learn.

The daily history of the Intellect is this alternating of expansions and concentrations. The expansions are the invitations from heaven to try a larger sweep, a higher pitch than we have yet climbed, and to leave all our past for this enlarged scope.[p. 118] Present power, on the other hand, requires concentration on the moment and the thing to be done.

The condition of sanity is to respect the order of the intellectual world; to keep down talent in its place, to enthrone the instinct. There must be perpetual rallying and self–recovery. Each talent is ambitious and self–asserting; it works for show and for the shop, and the greater it grows the more is the mischief and the misleading, so that presently all is wrong.

No wonder the children love masks and costumes, and play horse, play soldier, play school, play bear, and delight in theatricals. The children have only the instinct of the universe, in which becoming somewhat else is the perpetual game of nature, and death the penalty of standing still. 'T is not less in thought[p. 120]. I cannot conceive any good in a thought which confines and stagnates. The universe exists only in transit, or we behold it shooting the gulf from the past to the future. We are passing into new heavens in fact by the movement of our solar system, and in thought by our better knowledge. Transition is the attitude of power. A fact is only a fulcrum of the spirit. It is the terminus of a past thought, but only a means now to new sallies of the imagination and new progress of wisdom.

The habit of saliency, of not pausing but proceeding, is a sort of importation and domestication of the divine effort into a man. Routine, the rut, is the path of indolence, of cows, of sluggish animal life; as near gravitation as it can go. But wit sees the short way, puts together what belongs together, custom or no custom; in that is organization.

Inspiration is the continuation of the divine effort that built the man. The same course continues itself in the mind which we have witnessed in nature, [p. 122] namely the carrying–on and completion of the metamorphosis from grub to worm, from worm to fly. In human thought this process is often arrested for years and ages. The history of mankind is the history of arrested growth. This premature stop, I know not how, befalls most of us in early youth; as if the growth of high powers, the access to rare truths, closed at two or three years in the child, while all the pagan faculties went ripening on to sixty.

So long as you are capable of advance, so long you have not abdicated the hope and future of a divine soul. [p. 124] That wonderful oracle will reply when it is consulted, and there is no history or tradition, no rule of life or art or science, on which it is not a competent and the only competent judge.

Man was made for conflict, not for rest. In action is his power; not in his goals but in his transitions man is great. Instantly he is dwarfed by self–indulgence. The truest state of mind rested in becomes false.

The spiritual power of man is twofold, mind and heart, Intellect and morals; one respecting truth, the other the will. [p. 128] One is the man, the other the woman in spiritual nature. *One is power, the other is love.* [p. 128] These elements always coexist in every normal individual, but one predominates. And as each is easily exalted in our thoughts till it serves to fill the universe and become the synonym of God, the soul in which one predominates is ever watchful and jealous when such immense claims are made for one as seem injurious to the other. Ideal and practical, like ecliptic and equator, are never parallel. Each has its vices, its proper dangers, obvious enough when the opposite element is deficient.

Intellect is skeptical, runs down into talent, selfish working for private ends, conceited, ostentatious and malignant. On the other side the clear headed thinker complains of souls led hither and thither by affections which, alone, are blind guides and thriftless workmen, and in the confusion asks the polarity of intellect. But all great minds and all great hearts have mutually allowed the absolute necessity of the twain.

If the first rule is to obey your genius, in the second place the good mind is known by the choice of what is positive, of what is advancing. We must embrace the affirmative. But the affirmative of affirmatives is love.[p. 130] Quantus amor tantus animus.[37] Strength enters as the moral element enters. Lovers of men are as safe as the sun. Goodwill makes insight. Sensibility is the secret readiness to believe in all kinds of power, and the contempt of any experience we have not is the opposite pole. *The measure of mental health is the disposition to find good everywhere, good and order, analogy, health and benefit, — the love of truth, tendency to be in the right, no fighter for victory, no cockerel.*[p. 132] 38

We have all of us by nature a certain divination and parturient vaticination in our minds of some higher good and perfection than either power or knowledge.[p. 134] Knowledge is plainly to be preferred before power, as being that which guides and directs its blind force and impetus; but *Aristotle declares that the origin of reason is not reason but something better.*[p. 138]

The height of culture, the highest behavior, consists in the identification of the Ego with the universe; so that when a man says I hope, I find, I think, he might properly say, The human race thinks or finds or hopes.[p. 140] And meantime he shall be able continually to keep sight of his biographical Ego, — I have a desk, I have an office, I am hungry, I had an ague,[39] — as rhetoric or offset to his grand spiritual Ego, without impertinence, or ever confounding them.

I may well say this is divine, the continuation of the divine effort. Alas! it seems not to be ours, to be quite independent of us. Often there is so little affinity between the man and his works that we think the wind must have writ them.[p. 142] Also its communication from one to another follows its own law and refuses our intrusion. It is in one, it belongs to all; yet how to impart it?

We need all our resources to live in the world which is to be used and decorated by us. Socrates kept all his virtues as well as his faculties well in hand. He was sincerely humble, but he utilized his humanity chiefly as a better eyeglass to penetrate the vapors that baffled the vision of other men.

The superiority of the man is in the simplicity of his thought, that he has no obstruction, but looks straight at the pure fact, with no color of option. Profound sincerity is the only basis of talent as of character. The virtue of the Intellect is its own, its courage is of its own kind, and at last it will be justified, though for the moment it seem hostile to what it most reveres.[p. 144]

We wish to sum up the conflicting impressions by saying that all point at last to a unity which inspires all. Our poetry, our religion are its skirts and penumbrae. Yet the charm of life is the hints we derive from this. They overcome us like perfumes from a far–off shore of sweetness, and their meaning is that no tongue shall syllable it without leave; that only itself can name it; that by casting ourselves on it and being its voice it rushes each moment to positive commands, creating men and methods, and ties the will of a child to the love of the First Cause.[p. 146]

Notes

[1] Martin Buber (1878 – 1965), Jewish philosopher, translator, and educator, whose most famous work *Ich und Du* (1923) was translated into English as *I and Thou*. Martin Buber, *I and Thou* (New York: Charles Scribner's Sons, 1970).

[2] The street boys in Mumbai know that the best pickings are in the wealthy neighborhoods; the rich throw away so much. Julian Crandall–Hollick, *Life with India's Ragpickers,* National Public Radio, http://www.npr.org/templates/story/story.php?storyId=1139257 (Accessed November 9, 2008).

[3] Gottfried Wilhelm Leibnitz (1646–1716), German polymath: co–discover of calculus, discoverer of the binary mathematical system, philosopher.

[4] You can think of a monad as a mirrored sphere that reflects its surroundings in its perfectly mirrored surface. Each monad reflects, and in that sense contains, the whole of its environment.

[5] Friedrich Wilhelm Nietzsche (1844–1900), German philosopher and philologist who developed a style of radical questioning, and destroyed idealistic philosophy.

[6] Stephen Mitchell, *The Tao Te Ching: A new English version* (New York: Harper & Row, 1988).

[7] Eugene Wigner, "The unreasonable effectiveness of mathematics in the natural sciences," *Communications on Pure and Applied Mathematics* 13, no. 1 (1960): 1–14. http://www.dartmouth.edu/~matc/MathDrama/reading/Wigner.html (Accessed November 9, 2008).

[8] cf. Rudolf Steiner, *Goethe's Theory of Knowledge* (Herndon, VA: Steiner Books, 2008).

[9] George Boas, "Macrocosm and Microcosm," *The Dictionary of the History of Ideas*, Electronic Text Center at the University of Virginia Library, http://etext.virginia.edu/cgi-local/DHI/dhi.cgi?id=dv3-16 (Accessed November 9, 2008).

[10] Joseph Cornell, *Listening to Nature: How to Deepen Your Awareness of Nature* (Nevada City, CA: Dawn Publications, 1995).

[11] "The perceptual richness of words is for me not just pedantry. Each is unique, and saliently so. They all have different shapes and colors. And even though each letter of a word is colored differently, a word's color isn't simply made up of the colors of its component letters. The shades combine, bleed into each other, change slightly depending on their neighbors."—Karen Chenausky quoted at http://web.mit.edu/synesthesia/www/colordemo.html (Accessed November 9, 2008).

[12] Marius von Senden, *Space and sight: The perception of space and shape in the congenitally blind*

before and after operation (Glencoe, IL: Free Press, 1960).

[13] John Locke (1632 – 1704). English philosopher and the first British empiricist.

[14] Encyclopædia Britannica, "chemical bonding," Encyclopædia Britannica Online, http://search.eb.com/eb/article-43377 (Accessed November 9, 2008).

[15] Immanuel Kant (1724–1804). One of the most influential of German philosophers.

[16] Henri Bortoft, *The Wholeness of Nature* (Edinburgh, Scotland: Floris Books, 1996).

[17] Isabel Gauthier and Michael J. Tarr, "Becoming a 'greeble' expert: Exploring mechanisms for face recognition," *Vision Research* 37, no. 12 (1997): 1673–1682.

[18] Frederick Louis MacNeice (1907–1963). Irish poet and playwright.

[19] David Lloyd George (1863–1945) was the first and only British Prime Minister of Welsh ancestry, and the last Liberal to hold the office.

[20] Schizophrenia is a mental disorder characterized by abnormalities in the perception of reality. Common symptoms include auditory hallucinations, paranoid delusions, or disorganized speech and thinking.

[21] Anschluss (the accession), or Anschluss Österreichs (accession of Austria), was the Nazi annexation of Austria into Greater Germany. The entry of German troops into Austria on March 12, 1938 was greeted with jubilation by the majority of the Austrian populace.

[22] Kristallnacht (Crystal Night, but generally referred to as the Night of Broken Glass in English) was a coordinated attack in the form of a staged riot directed against the Jewish inhabitants of Germany by the Nazi Party on November 9 and 10, 1938. 95 Jews were killed and ca. 27,000 were arrested and sent to concentration camps. More than 200 Synagogues were destroyed in that single night.

[23] Pema Chödrön, *The Wisdom of No Escape* (Boston: Shambhala, 1991).

[24] Rudolf Steiner, *Verses and Meditations* (London: Rudolf Steiner Press, 1972), p. 223.

[25] Sir Richard Owen (1804–1892), English biologist, comparative anatomist and paleontologist, was the driving force behind the formation of the British Museum of Natural History.

[26] A Greek name given to the population who preceded the Hellenic peoples in Greece.

[27] A slave girl in *Uncle Tom's Cabin* by Harriet Beecher Stowe; published in 1852. The phrase "growed like Topsy" became a popular figure of speech used to describe something that grew without design or intention. See *The Word Detective*, May 20, 2003, http://www.word-detective.com/052003.html (Accessed November

9, 2008).

[28] Sir Kenelm Digby (1603 – 1665); physicist, naval commander (privateer), diplomatist and member of the first council of the Royal Society. Author of two philosophical treatises: "Nature of Bodies" and the "Immortality of Reasonable Souls".

[29] Brook Farm (1841–1847) was a utopian community organized by George and Sophia Ripley in West Roxbury, Massachusetts. Nathaniel Hawthorne was one of its most well known members.

[30] William Page (1811–1885), American painter and portrait artist.

[31] The priestess and Oracle of Apollo at Delphi delivered prophecies in a state of frenzy.

[32] A child lost to an single, isolated conviction.

[33] A rill is narrow, shallow incision into the soil caused by erosion resulting from water flow over uneven soil. Penury is excessive frugality. A penurious rill a shallow erosion ditch with little flow.

[34] A fragrant essential oil.

[35] A pastoral elegy written by John Milton in 1637, and published in 1638.

[36] Believe me, such an error has its own merit.

[37] How great is your love, of that size is your intellect.

[38] Cockerel: A rooster; a male chicken, under one year old; hence a person very full of him or herself.

[39] A fever with chills and sweating that occurs at regular intervals, as in malaria.

www.ingramcontent.com/pod-product-compliance
Lightning Source LLC
Chambersburg PA
CBHW041419290326
41932CB00042B/20